Nature's Quiet Conversations

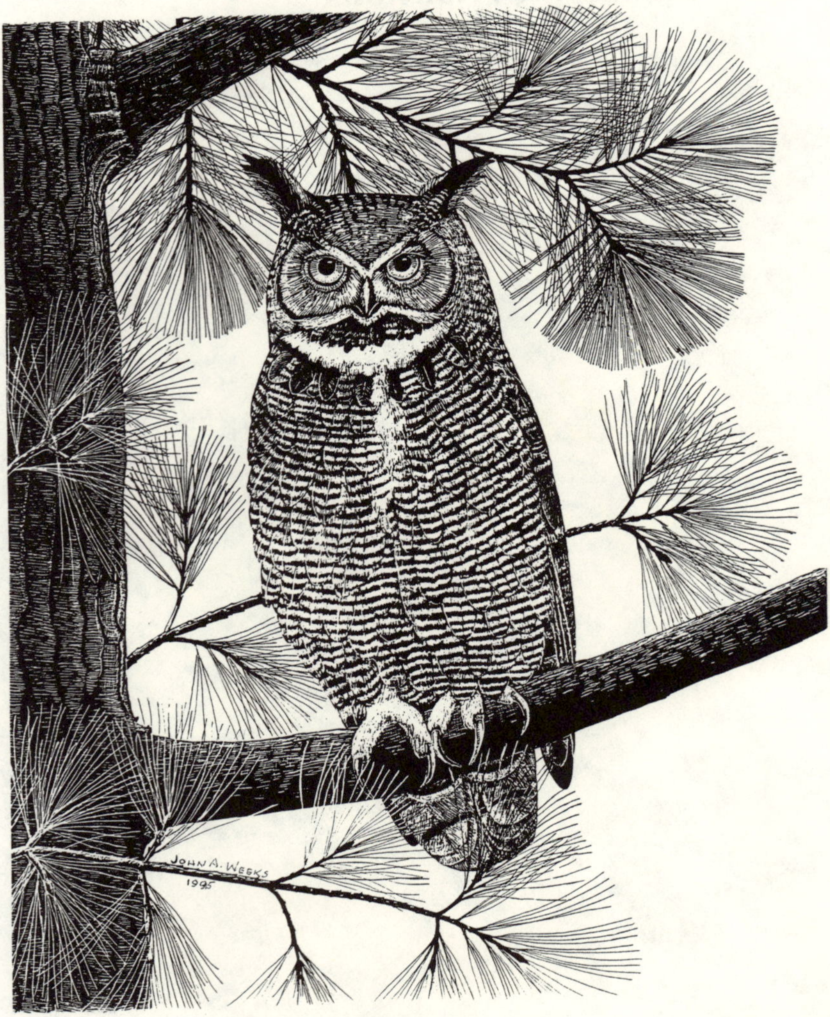
JOHN A. WEEKS
1995

Nature's Quiet Conversations

John A. Weeks

Edited by Janet J. Smith

Foreword by Donald D. Cox

To Kathy
"Keep It Natural"
John A. Weeks 5/18/13

DISTRIBUTED BY SYRACUSE UNIVERSITY PRESS

Copyright © 2006 by John A. Weeks
All Rights Reserved

First Edition 2006

06 07 08 09 10 11   6 5 4 3 2 1

The production of this book was made possible by a grant from Frank and Janet Smith through the Central New York Community Foundation to the Centers for Nature Education, Inc., at Baltimore Woods.

All sketches were drawn by the author.

The paper used in this publication meets the minimum requirements of American National Standard for Information Sciences—Permanence of Paper for Printed Library Materials, ANSI Z39.48–1984.∞™

ISBN-13: 978-0-8156-8150-2
ISBN-10: 0-8156-8150-X

Produced and distributed by Syracuse University Press
Syracuse, New York 13244–5160
www.SyracuseUniversityPress.syr.edu

Manufactured in the United States of America

To the memories of

Sarah A. Weeks

my mother, who taught me to admire

and cherish God's handiwork

and

Edwin J. Weeks

my father, who taught me to

aspire to excellence

John A. Weeks is widely recognized as a biologist, botanist, environmental educator, artist, author, and commentator. His weekly radio essays have been heard for twenty-four years on the region's public radio station, WRVO.

Contents

Illustrations   xi
Foreword, *Donald D. Cox*   xiii
Preface   xvii
Acknowledgments   xxi

Remembering

The Times They Are A-Changing   3
The First Best Walk of Spring   7
Cloud Watching   10
Viewing the Eternal Sunrise   13
The Rewards of a Winter Walk   16
A Return to Hallowed Grounds   19
Save That Apple Tree   22
The Little Creatures of Autumn   25
Alien Invaders   29
Half Steps in History   33
Opening Day and Buck Fever   37

Observing Spring

April Sunshine   43
The Springtime Juggernaut   46

Watching the Geese at Vann Road   49
The Courtship of Amphibians   52
Spring Thunder and a Native American   55
A Word in Defense of the Dandelion   58
The Romance of the Egg   61
Springtime Symphony   64
Honk Once If You Agree   67
The Calico Fields   70

Observing Summer

Touring Nature's Garden by Canoe   77
The Hummingbird! Minute, Mighty, Magical   81
The Sad Plight of the Bobolink   84
Nature's Predators Serve a Purpose   87
Butterflies That Flutter By   90
The Story of a Tree   93
The Continuing Story of a Tree   96
My August Walk in Baltimore Woods   99

Observing Autumn

September's Bittersweet Conversation   107
Twin Miracles of Flight and Frenzy   110
The Story of the Golden Meadows   113
An Autumn Less Than Grand Glorious   116
The Ebbing Tide of Migration   119
The Monarch: Our Most Unusual Migrant   122
The Loon   125
In Search of the Gobbler's Tale   128
November's Dialogue   132

Observing Winter

    The Texture of Winter   137

    White Shadow of the Woods   140

    Feeder Talk   143

    The Bald Eagle   147

    Reynard! Red Menace or Worthy Citizen?   150

    Happy New Year, Gregorian and Natural   154

    The January-Spring Syndrome   157

    What the Groundhog Told Me   160

Conserving

    On Appreciating Death   165

    Recycling and the Honey Wagon   169

    The Changing Seasons   172

    CO_2 and the Next Ice Age   175

    Creating an Environmental Bill of Rights   178

    A Message from a Pretty Gifted Grosbeak   181

    Spotted Owl: Issue or Icon?   184

    The Last Setting of the Table   187

    Annual Four-Minute Environmental Teach-In   190

Index   193

Illustrations

Great horned owl   *frontispiece*
Flooded field   4
View of the farm   7
Pileated woodpecker   18
Baltimore oriole   23
Chickadee and corn   27
Ring-necked pheasant   30
Black bear   34
Buck   39
Hepatica   44
Mushrooms   46
Flying geese   51
Ruffed grouse drumming   56
Bluebird in sugar maple   63
Red-winged blackbird   66
Wetland scene   78
Hummingbird and columbine   82
Bobcat   88

Blue jay   94
Wood thrush   100
Robin on sumac   108
Monarch and day lily   123
Loon   127
Wild turkey   130
Varying hare   138
Long-tailed weasel   140
Winter feeder   144
Red fox   152
Horned owl   155
Groundhog   161
Central New York nature areas   166
White-tailed deer   173
Flying geese   188
Red trillium and squirrel corn   192

Foreword

Donald D. Cox

There are many books in print that are loaded with facts and figures about the natural world. Their objective usually is to present the facts accurately. John Weeks's *Nature's Quiet Conversations* includes an abundance of facts and figures, but unlike most of the others the objective of this book is not simply to present the facts but to interpret them in terms of the ecosystem. It is elegantly written in simple, often poetic prose that even the most technically challenged individual can read and understand. John Weeks is well known in central New York as a nature artist. *Nature's Quiet Conversations* has thirty-four illustrations, but it is an understatement to refer to them merely as illustrations; each is a work of art.

In our very busy lives as we rush to and from work or on errands for our spouse or our children, or for other activities that seem important to us, we may miss the drama of nature that may be taking place in our backyard or the vacant lot next door. Even if we observe a natural event we are likely not to recognize its significance in the fabric of the ecosystem. There is a tendency to place more emphasis on events that occur in summer, as if this is the time most things occur, but natural history is not seasonal. There are events that take place in winter that are as compelling as any that occur in summer. Nor is the size of the participant in a natural event an indication of its importance. This book includes a series of essays on each of the seasons that address these observations. I characterize each essay as a "mini eco-story." They have enticing titles such as "The Little Creatures of Autumn," "Alien Invaders," and "The Sad Plight of the Bobolink." To the lover of nature each title evokes stimulation to read further to see what secret will be revealed.

The natural world is very complex in structure. No single book can give a clear picture of all aspects of native ecosystems. Each of the "mini eco-stories" provides a tantalizing window into one corner of the ecosystem. Through these windows one gets a glimpse of some very complex ecological principles such as productivity, energy cycles, and food webs. Many of the essays challenge the reader to think outside the box. Consider the concept of the texture of winter or the idea that November is one of our most talkative months if you can learn the language. On the practical side the book is organized into short independent narratives. If you have only a short time before you must rush off on an errand, you will have time to finish a story. Then you will have something pleasant to think about until you get back to read the next section.

We are living in a time when the world is changing at an accelerating rate. The world I knew in my youth and that John Weeks knew in his youth is gone forever. The human population continues to grow unchecked along with the many associated problems. Among these are the progressive destruction of natural habitats and the increasing number of endangered and extinct species. Wetlands continue to be destroyed at a rate of about 5 percent per year. Water and air pollution are at record levels, and acid rain continues to devastate sensitive areas. The disaster of global warming is almost a certainty, even if preventive measures are initiated today. All of these are ecological problems, and human civilization, as we know it, depends on whether or not we find solutions. These should have top priority in our social, economic, and political lives. In the section of the book entitled "Conserving," problems of this scope are analyzed with a depth of understanding that comes only from a lifetime of observation and study.

In *A Sand County Almanac* Aldo Leopold wrote elegantly about the ecological problems of his day. Since that time the population of the earth has doubled, technology has doubled several times, and environmental problems have escalated to become global. In *Nature's Quiet Conversations*, John Weeks, in language that is equally elegant, addresses the ecological problems of today. The message in his book is clear; it is a plea for people to wake up and to take steps immediately to save our living environment before it is too late.

Preface

Down I ramble, through the forest that fills my heart with sheer gladness, tasting the freshness, the quiet that surrounds me; almost drinking from the heavy mist as it is so pervaded by this feeling. When I walk among the tall, stately firs, and oaks, I perceive no boundaries that can hold me, not even the restlessness of my own mind, as it becomes subdued in this calm. Now and then I pause for a closer look at a delicate fern or small woodland flower. The trees cause me to walk tall, the air bids me to breathe slow and deep; every living thing calls me to investigate it, discover the incredible handiwork of its master. Again and again, I'm held in speechless awe at the marvel of this forest, a place whose healing is, for me, unequaled. This place, the forest, seems to have reached into my very blood, always calling me back to roam its unmarked halls. And to lay at rest on moss-covered stream banks, in deep gratefulness to the Creator of it all. —JWD

Anyone who was born in the Roaring Twenties, whose youth spanned the great depression and World War II, whose young adult life encompassed the sometimes maligned but fondly remembered fifties and whose influence on the minds of others began to mature in the reactionary sixties, has surely witnessed a peaceful lifestyle revolution in a land founded on revolution of a different kind.

Such life experience is unlikely to produce a person whose heart and professional activity reflect the great natural history movements of the eighteenth and nineteenth centuries, but it had that effect on me. This book explains why my early heroes were Agassiz, Audubon, and Thoreau and why I maintain that their messages as updated by the great nature writers of our time are vital to the well-being of the twenty-first-century world.

My youth was awash with nature-related influences. Both of my parents, in their own way, projected a love for nature. My mother was gifted both at writing and reciting. Her passion for expressing her love for God's creation made an early and lasting impression. My father, a professional artist, though less passionate about it in his own artwork and his speech, captured the essence of what motivated my mother. He also let it be understood early that he had no secret goals for my life. He expected me to do whatever I chose with honesty and a devotion to excellence, no compromise.

All of my five siblings caught some of the fire that motivated me, but I had the good fortune of being the youngest. Ed, Eleanore, Bill, Dorothy, and Jean provided me with my own cohort of unfailingly supportive allies.

That was fortunate because there was little in the makeup of my hometown to nourish my specific interest except my next-door neighbor, Carl I. Bergerson, superintendent of schools. There was also the village librarian, Miss Achilles, whom we boys considered stern and unsmiling, but who was extremely helpful to those in whom she saw promise. She introduced me to the literature, which my mother, the gifted reciter, helped to invest with compelling dimensions.

Then there was my older brother Ed, who took the time to introduce me in minute detail to the world around me. Ed showed me my first bird's nest, my first bluebird, and so many other important firsts that he rivaled my three and one half years at Cornell and my two years at Syracuse. Brother Ed was my first and best professor.

All of this insured that my preoccupation for wild things did not preclude an interest in people and their reactions to my beloved wild world. I was, in my youth, hunter, fisherman, and agriculturist. My adult mentors included sportsmen and farmers. I learned about husbandry and about exploitation from them. Still, the thing that cemented my lifelong dedication to natural history was the hours I spent in the field, mostly by myself but occasionally with select pals whose interest was not so much in nature as it was in being buddies and helpers.

It is probably fortunate that my brother was not always available to answer questions and that his professorial bent generally lead him to propound spin-off questions rather than direct answers. I learned to research. A day in the woods could lead to hours, even days of reading.

My formal education provided further stimulus. Even in public school, I began to get a sense of the factors at work that were influencing my natural workshop. The modest growth of my hometown brought about changes to my favored haunts that early troubled me. Infusing all of this was a deep and growing religious faith, initiated by my parents but nourished by my dialogues with the people I admired most.

My professional life as wildlife biologist, college teacher, and founder and administrator of nature education centers provided both need and opportunity for the creation of these chronicles. This book is neither religious nor environmental exhortation. It is rather a witness to what I have seen and believed. It is a gentle reminder that nature is still the main provider of all of our wealth, both material and spiritual.

There is constant need for translators who can interpret and transpose nature's messages in a way that catches the attention of the environmentally deaf and blind. For nearly twenty-four years, I have made a modest attempt to keep the dialogue alive through weekly five-minute radio programs. This book draws on those programs to reveal the inspiration and the inner workings of nature and to remind everyone how important it is to "Keep It Natural."

Some of these essays, written decades ago, may seem to ignore important subsequent environmental changes. We have decided not to update them, but to print them as originally written.

Acknowledgments

I have emphasized elsewhere in this book how important my family has been in providing the spark that ignited a lifelong interest in nature and in its literature. They did not, however, ever suggest to me that I should become a nature writer.

The encouragement for that came from the requirements of my work and from the encouragement of my newspaper editors through the years to make my columns more than just progress reports from the Rogers Center at Sherburne and Beaver Lake Nature Center near Baldwinsville, New York. While I feel some debt to all of the editors with whom I have worked, two, Marge Chase, former editor of the *Norwich Sun* and Al Baker, former editor of the *Baldwinsville Messenger* and the Brown Newspaper Chain stand out because of the length and the productivity of those relationships.

I feel an equal sense of obligation to every staff member of WRVO at Oswego for outstanding cooperative efforts and support, both professional and personal. Perhaps here I should avoid names because I can't possibly mention everyone, but I can't resist the inclination to thank John Hurlbutt, program director, who first agreed to give the radio spot a chance and put up with a lot of mediocrity until the *Nature of Things* hit its stride. I've worked with a number of operations directors, all extremely helpful, but Jane Kelly deserves recognition for helping in my desire to expand the scope of my efforts. Station managers Bill Shigley and John Krauss have been unfailingly supportive.

In one of the essays, I describe my five children, Denise, Gary, Brenda, Joni, and Donald, as semiprecious commodities. Actually they, and my wife Esther, have patiently put up with an occasionally preoccupied husband and father and have helped to make the process of learning great fun. That's precious.

Last of all, I am deeply indebted to those directly involved in the production of the book. My daughter Brenda Weeks has reviewed the articles and provided excellent suggestions about syntax and clarity of expressions. Similarly Greg Smith, chief naturalist at Beaver Lake, has done a superb job of checking for scientific accuracy and helped to update articles, some of which were written over twenty years ago.

I had hoped to include some of the sensitive verse written by my mother, but I was unable to locate any appropriate examples. During the search, I happened upon some verse written by my daughter Joni Weeks Dyer and found in it an uncanny reincarnation of my mother's insightful thoughts. I present snippets here (with the attribution of JWD), with great pride.

Georgia Gillespie and Janet Smith share the credit for initiating this book project. Janet, in particular, has been unstinting in performing the detailed work of making the essays ready for presentation to the publisher.

Remembering

In the deep stillness of the evening
When naught but the loon
Honking at the lake's edge
Breaks the silence,
I pause to take stock
    of all that has come and gone
    that day. —JWD

Nature has a broad appeal, but natural history as a profession attracts only a few. Full-time careers in this field are rare, the financial rewards modest. Even so, the competition for jobs is lively, and many who aspire to that career find themselves shunted into related fields.

My careers as a college biology teacher and nature center administrator formed only a partial distraction. My natural history roots were too deep. What was occasional recreation for some was habit for me. I spent most of my spare time in the field; observing, writing and sketching, and heightening my awareness of the gradual change that was occurring.

Civilization trades on the raw material of the environment, and the maintenance of a world that is both nourishing and inspirational takes planning and commitment. However, our environmental memories are flawed. Even some committed naturalists have difficulty in keeping track of change. If we don't keep notes, we have difficulty remembering what things were like yesterday, let alone last year or in the last decade. If our perception of change is this weak, we are not likely to give much thought to the implications of change.

In the Remembering section of this book, I have included a few essays that will take you back in time to share with me the joy of discovery.

The Times They Are A–Changing

I grew up in what I presume is one of the flatter parts of New York State, the lake plains of Orleans County west of Rochester. It was a good enough place for a budding naturalist with its lakeshore marshes, inlets, and estuaries: the rank marshlands along the lower reaches of Oak Orchard Creek, for instance. Then across the county in the southwest corner were those wetlands now incorporated into the Oak Orchard Wildlife Management Area and the Iroquois National Wildlife Refuge.

Between these extremes were acres and acres of diversified farmlands, apple, peach, and cherry orchards and a plethora of tiny woodlots, most of them less than ten acres in size but withal rich in birdlife, especially songbirds. The marshlands introduced me to gallinule, now called the moorhen, sora and Virginia rail, least bittern, American bittern, and green heron. I found the nest sites of black ducks, blue-winged teal, and at that time the rarer wood duck and mallard. Best of all, the orchards and the pasture fences harbored enough bluebirds to inspire any bird lover.

But it isn't any of those regular habitat complexes that come to mind when I think of the springtimes of my youth. It is the annual flooding of the lowland fields along the drainage channels that stirs up memories.

First there was the invasion of sea gulls as we called them. They descended in huge numbers upon temporary lakes that developed when the first warm rains of spring began to erode the deep blanket

First aired on WRVO-FM, Feb. 21, 1986.

of snow. It was not unusual to go to bed tired out from slogging through slushy snows and to awake to find my tracks obliterated by a ten-acre lake across the midsection of the farm. The just barely inundated stubble of corn, cabbage, and soy beans or the debris from a tomato field provided a wealth of foraging for the gulls. More often than not, the gulls were accompanied by waterfowl, handsome pintails and American wigeon in their finest nuptial dress. It was the only time in the whole year when I could find these species within ten miles of my home ground.

This lake might persist for only a day or two, never longer than a week. Normally it was a March phenomenon because if the heavy rains delayed until April there was seldom enough snow left to fuel the flood tide. It wasn't just the wildlife that attracted me there. With my friends, I attempted a hundred hydraulic engineering projects creating a low earthen dam here, a drainage ditch there, our own

It was not unusual to awake to find my tracks obliterated by a ten-acre pond.

small impoundments or drainage projects just to watch the water flow.

Sometimes we launched homemade sailboats and followed them across the shallow seas. Many times we got stuck in the mud, occasionally so deeply mired that we had to be rescued. Sometimes we just watched our boats from the shoreline as they drifted across the embayments slowly seeking out the drainage channel. Once in the channel, they would scoot along until they found the churning outlet thence to swoop in a great arc around the orchards so swiftly that we had to run to keep up.

We didn't really have to retrieve the boats until they reached the long low culvert that traversed the highway. If we didn't catch them by then, they were lost to us, for the culvert entered the fenced-in canning factory grounds where tomatoes and peas would be processed in another season. By canning time, the water had drained from the fields so that they could be plowed, fitted, and planted. The wildlife would have changed completely, too. It would be nothing then to find a bobolink or a meadowlark's nest where just a month and a half earlier gulls and waterfowl, even one of our toy boats, had drifted.

In those days, everyone knew the lowlands were periodically flooded and no one would have thought to put anything more permanent than a makeshift toolshed or a crib there. Today the midsection of that old farm is covered with houses, and I am forced to wonder what kind of elaborate or expensive provisions had to be made to deal with the periodic flooding.

I've never been back to those particular acres to see, but I'll bet on rainy spring days there are a lot of sump pumps going to rid the basements of stray flood waters. One thing is sure, there are no more handsome pintails or raucous gulls there to greet the spring freshet. No more orchards to attract the bluebirds. No more vesper sparrows to move into the fallow fields to set up housekeeping as soon as the water receded.

Now I wonder, if in one of those dozens of look-alike houses there is a young lad of eight or nine who finds his inspiration in meadowlark or meadow vole or oxeye daisy, where does he go to watch nature at work? The times they are a-changing, and the ghosts of Ed Weeks, my conservationist brother, or Stuart Flintham, the great forester who wrote so movingly of his field excursions in those acres a generation earlier, have lost their environmental birthright without even knowing it was happening. Progress is sometimes hard on naturalists.

The First Best Walk of Spring

The second Monday in April this year ranked with the best I can remember from those blessed days of my youth when no activity could take priority over a walk through the fields and woodlot of the home farm. Somehow or other, I could always find enough time for a meander through some appropriate portion of the varied habitat of that late 1930s farm on which I grew up. Its hedgerows, drainage course, low-lying crop fields, orchards, and shrub-covered odd corners were ideal for wild things year-round or in migration.

First aired on WRVO-FM, Apr. 12, 1991.

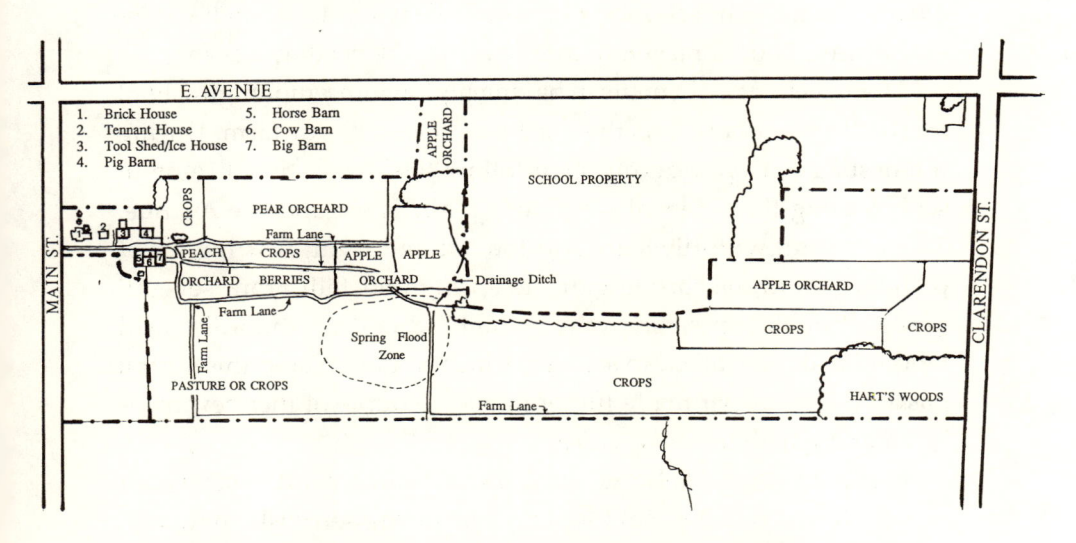

The farm's hedgerows, drainage course, low-lying crop fields, orchards and shrub-covered corners were ideal for wild things year around or in migration.

A direct path to school, a half mile away, led me past barns, a copse of chokecherry, an aged but still producing pear orchard to the north and a very young peach orchard to the south. It then passed by a swath of crop fields and berry patches and finally traversed apple orchards of age-old greenings, maiden blush, Baldwins, kings, and Rome beauties. The last few yards before my pathway entered the school property, which had been carved from our own back acres, took me across the main drainage channel that made farming of the lowlands possible.

There were times in a wet spring when this last section could be impassable to anyone who lacked at least knee-high boots. This might require a quarter-mile detour to the south to a place where the farm lane crossed the ditch, but even those quarter-mile detours could provide enrichment of remarkable dimensions. To the north, a quarter-mile diversion could lead me past the pig yard through a copse where cuckoos and catbirds nested or bring me to the north property line, which was also the back line of the houses along East Avenue in town. The edge between backyards and pear orchard always produced oriole, wren, chipping sparrow, and hummingbird. Near the edge of the school grounds was the wettest part of the property, always good for a yellowthroat during the nesting season.

There were daily benefits in having junior and senior high school located in what once was the northeast corner of our farm. During the nesting season, I didn't often follow the conventional route to school along the sidewalks of South Main Street and the Avenue. This shortcut, with diversions to the left and right, was my usual pathway to school throughout the spring and fall. From seventh grade through my senior year in high school, my buddies with whom I usually walked to school seemed to understand this spring passion. They never made fun of it, and a couple of them even enjoyed going with me on occasion.

It might sound like I was an indifferent student, often tardy and usually distracted. Not so! I took my schooling seriously and actually excelled. My family, mother, father, and older brothers and sisters, expected that of me. There was a friendly pressure there for which I was later grateful. I paid attention to my English, Latin, and math as well as my sciences.

Today, even with the pressures of other responsibilities, I treasure the early spring walks in search of the first flowers of spring and the migrating birds. Just this morning I got out soon after sunup in search of spring. What I found along the trails of Baltimore Woods was white, pink, and blue hepatica, the hallmark of spring there, and dainty spring beauties, their white petals liberally marked with pink tracery. Yellow coltsfoot at the edge of the Faust Garden was blooming beside a lone daphne that, after five years of abuse by browsing deer, wore a protective sheath of chicken wire through this winter. It is now covered with lilac blooms. Cohosh and leek are also prominent, and here and there are trilliums, some already budded. We'll see an eruption of flowers soon if the mild weather continues.

It's also a perfect time for those of you who have damp, semi-brushy fields nearby to go out just before nightfall to observe the courtship flight of the woodcock. Get there at dusk, and if you have any of the strange little birds present you will hear their miniature Bronx cheers followed by the whistling of wings as the bird circles upward in flight. If you are fortunate enough to find them, try to follow their zigzag descent to the ground. Their performance on the ground is every bit as interesting as their aerial maneuvering.

On this morning, the most interesting birds I observed were song sparrows getting ready to nest and golden-crowned kinglets busily plying the hemlocks beside the Overlook Trail. These tiny birds, smaller than a house wren, are olive drab above and white below with striking yellow or orange crowns margined with black and white streaks. They never seem to take time to rest. They work the hemlock boughs in search of insects and insect eggs, pausing only to utter their feeble grace notes. They paid little notice of me, so I watched them for some time before taking off again down the trail to my car. I had work to do, too.

Cloud Watching

Most of my life I've been a cloud watcher. It started when I was quite young, just old enough to be able to see fanciful images in the burgeoning cumulus clouds. I would lay on my back, eyes fixed on the swirling mass where great steeds and heroic riders emerged and melted away.

Sometimes the scenes where more contemporary, if no less fanciful; bucolic scenes with trees and shrubs and occasionally free-form wildlife. Often I wondered about the origin of this miraculous natural artistry. Did I will the clouds to take those forms, or were they God's gift to me? It never occurred to me that I might be tracing my own fancies upon that fibrous canvas; that someone else might look at the same scene and see something entirely different in it.

When I became a Boy Scout, my cloud watching took on a new dimension spurred on by an interested scoutmaster and the drawings by Eric Sloan in the original edition of the scout manual. That was one of the greatest books for youth ever published. It had Louis Agassiz Fuertes's line drawings of birds and Sloan's illustrations. There was the presence of Dan Beard who founded the Boy Scouts of America. I'm not sure whether "Green Bar Bill" Hillcourt, famous for his how-to-do-it books on nature activities, had a hand in that early edition, but I was soon aware of his great contribution to my life. I was thrilled years later to make his acquaintance.

It was Sloan's drawings of clouds comparing them to anvils, puffs of cotton, feathers, and twist on a stick that enabled me for the

First aired on WRVO-FM, July 27, 1990.

first time to distinguish between clouds: the building cumulonimbus, the fair weather cumulus, the puffs of altocumulus, the wisps of cirrus, and the rolls of stratocumulus.

I had only a fuzzy idea of how all of these related to the weather, even though the manual was quite specific about it. It didn't serve my needs at that time to be able to predict weather. An incipient naturalist dotes on change, and with the possible exception of the effect it had on early ground-nesting birds, my philosophy was, "Let it rain. I'll dry off when the sun comes out."

As a result of observing a bank of clouds and noting that individual elements moved in separate directions, I became aware of layering, and of the great differences in elevation of the layers. A thundery or stormy sky replete with low, middle, and high clouds was a wondrous thing. At sunset, the retreating sun highlighted successive layers by deserting and therefore darkening each tier starting with the lowest and moving upward. Shades of purple, pink, and gold shifted upward, and I always treasured that magic moment before the last fingers of gold deserted the high cirrus and each layer still maintained its own identity for a short time.

By following an accelerated junior high program, I missed earth science, but I learned through scouts and reading about the physics of cloud formation, absolute humidity, dewpoint, and nuclei of condensation, not to mention convection, radiation, and precipitation. I knew the physical principles, but I still saw images in the clouds.

Then after a semester at Cornell, I went into the service and wonder of wonders was accepted in the Army Air Corps weather unit. My familiarity with clouds and their implications grew as I learned about pressure systems, fronts, and the differences between polar and tropical, marine and continental air masses.

In addition, I got to watch cloud genesis in North Carolina, the Texas Panhandle, North Africa, and the Persian Gulf. I'm not sure whether it is any commentary on my ability as an observer and foreteller of weather that I moved to progressively easier places in terms of weather prediction. I remember a stretch of weeks in Arabia when there wasn't a single overcast day and only a few of broken cloud cover. Still I enjoyed the experience of sending up a weather balloon and confirming mathematically what I could surmise by estimating cloud height and observing differential cloud movements. Since then every significant change in cloud cover draws my attention and occasions a new wave of reminiscence.

Clouds, innocent products of atmospheric conditions, play their role in maintaining humid heat at night and depressing temperature buildup during the day. A study of clouds can help explain many things about local weather phenomena, and at the same time, feed your fancy and your appetite for that which is beautiful in nature.

> *The earth*
>   *an eye*
> *whose rains are tears*
>   *to wash her skies.* —JWD

Viewing the Eternal Sunrise

This is the story of a brief return to the country of my youth in search of the answer to a question: Have sunrises changed in the last forty years, or is the change really in me?

Today I'm propelled by a smoothly operating front-wheel-drive car. Then the power might have been a model A Ford coupe or a 1933 Essex. It doesn't matter which. After all, that was forty years ago. I head toward the black north country fringing Lake Ontario. I've watched the sun come up from this vantage point before. It should be a good place from which to make my comparison.

This is flat land, offering a broad panorama of roadside fields terminated in every direction by hedgerows or woodlots. There are no distant snow-clad hills or mountains. It would be a dull expanse, indeed, if it weren't for the variety of shapes and heights of the trees and the inevitable complex of barns and silos that project above the tree line at measured intervals.

I pull up to a well-remembered spot and look across a landscape I've known before but not seen for years. It's a still, frigid atmosphere with images so clear they wipe out all sense of distance. Objects several miles away are as sharp as those at roadside.

I study the eastern horizon for a moment, committing it all to memory, so that I'm able to superimpose this moment upon subsequent ones. That's the real secret of sunrise watching, after all; not the single moment viewed and forgotten, but the interplay of many moments, no two alike no matter how close together. The difference is comparable to that between a single shot of a rosebud and a time-

First aired on WRVO-FM, Mar. 3, 1989.

lapse sequence in which we see the bud opening, smoothly, inexorably, and magically becoming a full rose. If you have never studied a sunrise to see it unfold like the rosebud, I maintain you've never truly seen a sunrise.

Let's watch now as long as the brilliantly clear air will allow. Imagine first a small golden-scarlet arc still too narrow to silhouette the full crowns of the maples at the horizon. See it grow, reaching out to encompass nearly a third of the eastern horizon. All the time the fire at the center is warming like the fanned embers of last night's campfire. Its emanations expose details heretofore hidden within the lingering gray of night. Wisps of narrow clouds as fine and fibrous as a feather provide a charcoal-gray herringbone texture against the glowing atmosphere. As the sun rises and its fire spreads, the grays soften and warm. Soon the full light reaches them and they spring to life, pale gold now against a still pink background.

Now we realize that there are a few puffs of more substantial lower clouds, nascent cumulus. Strangely, their silhouettes have a purple cast at the edge. Soon these too will spring to life as the sun continues to mount. Finally the sun appears, a small white semicircle at the eastern horizon. The sky is aglow, a visual symphony of hot pink and gold neatly accented by evanescent purple traceries.

It's time to turn our back to the sun. Events of interest are beginning to appear in the west. The barren hardwoods, energized by the sun, show forth in shades of brown, gray, or gold as maple, beech, and willow begin to show their true natures. By contrast, pines and spruce seem to darken and recede. At one point, a grove of tall spruce emerges like a crowd of dark steeples. In another direction, a streamside fringe of willow shines forth like fine old gold. At intervals the plain geometry of human architecture intrudes upon the rustic tapestry.

At the base of the trees and varying across the intervening fields are dainty silver traceries where the sun strikes the far rims of the track of fox, skunk, and cottontail. These fine silver lines interweave in seemingly random but undoubtedly purposeful fashion.

As the moments wear on, another dramatic metamorphosis occurs. The cold blue shadows retreat across the snow-clad fields. The thin silver trails merge with the broader wind sculptured contours of the snow blanket, creating a new symphony in blue and silver. After a fleeting moment, this, too, is gone leaving only the daylight landscape punctuated here and there by hints of pearl, pink, gold, or purple.

What a show for the sensitive soul! The January sunrise is not an event but a process, a living, changing tapestry that signifies the start of a new day. One hour of twenty four, and yet for that day, no other hour will match it for dynamic beauty, unless the setting sun in a moment of recollection replays its mirror image.

That's the answer to my question, isn't it? The world around me may have changed completely, but the sun, like the rose, is still the sun. It can work its magic on these abandoned acres, just as it did when they were alive with farming activity. I may be forty years older, but the years have only taught me to appreciate every nuance of the sunrise. Its beauty is, indeed, eternal and universal.

The Rewards of a Winter Walk

I am delighted that an ever increasing number of people are learning to get out and enjoy the winter world. I can recall back in the early days as director of the Rogers Center at Sherburne, how we struggled to get a few people to break the winter pact they had made with hearthside and easy chair.

A few cross-country skiers, a few snowshoers, and an occasional backpacker would turn out for such events as owl howls, big-game safaris, and bushwhacking. Those programs consisted of howling at owls, following little tracks, and using the enabling bridges of ice and snow to visit otherwise inaccessible spots. These were good outings, but hardly anyone is left, I would guess, who still remembers. In those days backpacking was actually more popular than cross-country skiing. The participants were few but rugged.

I remember, especially, the first winter we had heat in the dormitory at Sherburne. A group of hikers from New York City and Long Island who were holding a retreat there were snowed in, cooped up in a winter wonderland. These were people prepared to challenge whatever winter offered. They even wanted to take a hike in the middle of a blizzard. We did, but many of those hearty souls dropped out before we'd made the two-thirds-of-a-mile circuit of the main trail loop. Of course, in those conditions, trails didn't mean much, nor did ponds or wetlands. We wandered a serendipitous route.

Some said afterwards they had never, until that moment, really

First aired on WRVO-FM, Jan. 14, 1988.

appreciated the relief offered by the lee side of a shrub packed with snow or of an arborvitae hedge similarly festooned. It wasn't hard to understand why deer, coon, or partridge were reluctant to leave their sheltered retreats in such conditions.

What a difference twenty-four hours can make. The next morning dawned bright and sunny exposing a real fairyland. We retraced our steps, finding little evidence that we had been there the day before. Every shrub and tree wore a white cap, pulled low to the windward. Every tree trunk supported a vertical column of snow plastered tight to the windward surface of the trunk. Pine, spruce, and cedar were well covered, their branches bending low with the added weight. It was indeed beautiful and exhilarating. Cameras clicked and people spoke in subdued tones, awed by the beauty.

Wildlife had not waited long after the passing of the storm to get out and explore. Rest days are not taken by wildlife without some loss. They work long hours without holidays to ensure survival. On this day, the deep snow wore an intricate tracery of rabbit tracks. Here we discovered where a rabbit had dined on the seeds of a buttonbush. In another spot, the object of attention was milkweed. Untouched seeds and the absence of down made us wonder what the rabbit actually ate. I voted for seeds but some of the group were certain the rabbit had actually eaten the down.

Rabbits weren't all that were moving, either. We found evidence out on the marsh where two cock pheasants had been tuning up their jousting skills preparing for the territorial battles of spring. Most of this contest is really just shadow boxing, but we did find a few burnished maroon feathers in the snow. Later on, from the gallery window, we saw the pair dining with several hens at the base of a buttonbush. Peace reigned now where a few hours earlier war games had been the order of the hour.

The best moment of that outing came along the river trail when a ruffed grouse erupted from a snowbank where it had apparently waited out the storm in the security of its own little snow cave. It took off with a shower of snow and a thunder of wings. It was the only time in years of leading winter walks that a group of people had

The second most memorable event of our post-blizzard walk was seeing a pileated woodpecker.

observed this common occurrence with me. I told them of the time in the Brookfield Forest area when I had encountered a grouse apparently trapped in the snow by a crust of ice. Only its head protruded from a hole too small for its body. With a sturdy arrowwood stave, I carefully removed the entrapping ice cap. The grouse in its haste to be elsewhere didn't pause to thank me.

The second most memorable event of our post-blizzard walk was a pileated woodpecker that came directly toward us across the Chenango River. I had spotted it afar and pointed it out, but my companions were sure it was just a crow. It was great to see their eyes widen in amazement as the bird approached. The pileated has that effect on people. It landed in a basswood perhaps thirty feet away, loudly protesting our intrusion into its domain. Its scarlet crest was raised as if to emphasize its dismay.

I hope that if you get out to ski or snowshoe or just to slog about, you'll get off the beaten path and search for signs of wild company.

A Return to Hallowed Grounds

They say you can't return, and in a way they are right. Oh, you can come back to the ancestral coordinates, but the latitude and longitude are about the only things that remain the same.

My old stomping grounds included typical Orleans County acres. That means flat, combined of orchard, row crop fields, and in the days of my youth, pasture. Woodlands were usually reduced to a minimum, less than five acres in the case of the farm on which I grew up. I was lucky, however, for the woodlots of two neighboring farms touched, creating perhaps fifteen acres of woodland known in those days as Hart's and Ryan's Woods or more traditionally just Hart's Woods.

These few acres were the spawning ground of my growing interest in natural history. The area had that tradition. I found that out during my senior year in high school when a kind and helpful librarian showed me a copy of the diary of Stuart Flintham, a forester who had spent his youth around the turn of the century studying those same acres. His beautifully written account of his observations helped to flesh out my own understanding of what I was observing. Thus Flintham joined Burroughs, Emerson, Thoreau, and Audubon in my inspiration bank. Unlike the others, however, he helped me cement in my mind specific recollections of my ancestral land. I remember these: the cutover beech-maple stand that wood thrush and vireo found so attractive; the low-flying copse of aspen, soft maple,

Originally published in the *Baldwinsville Messenger*, Aug. 2, 1978. First aired on WRVO-FM, Aug. 30, 2002.

and hornbeam beloved of redstart and catbird; the ragged weedy border where the woodcock performed his courtship flight and later nested; and the more mature woodlot across the fence line where I found the nests of ovenbird and veery.

In winter it had a bleaker aspect, except where the tangles of grapevine provided shelter and food for local birdlife as well as for hosts of visitors from the north. I could always count on finding a gaggle of roosting pheasants, even in the depth of winter, if I traveled to those grapevines just at sundown and trained my flashlight on its gloomy depths.

Sometimes we naturalists gain the reputation of being misanthropes, but my study of Hart's Woods and its surrounding croplands was not entirely a lonely adventure. I had a good friend who shared many hours there with me. He was not as interested in the natural history as I, but he was my buddy and we did things together. At times the whole gang enjoyed the woods. It was our campsite. From school-out to school-in, we pitched our tents and spent the good nights under the green canopy. We made a dozen abortive attempts at cabin building, spent hours polishing our scout woodcraft skills, and played a variety of games. A perfect day was one in which the spiraling glissando of the veery produced the invocation and the flutelike tremolos and grace notes of the wood thrush pronounced the benediction over our heads.

Imagine my delight, then, on a visit to my hometown when I read in the paper that the woods, now neighbor to an elementary school, were to be the object of a Youth Conservation Corps project to develop a nature center for the community. This seemed most appropriate to me. After all, nature centers are my business.

I had visited the area several times in recent years with my brother Ed, who had designed a nature trail there. I was pleased that the years had worked so few ravages on its natural attributes. It still was graced at dawn and sunset by the litanies of veery and wood thrush. Catbirds still nested in the grapevine tangles, and redstarts, grown scarce in recent years, still placed their exquisite felted cups in the vertical crotches of saplings.

On visiting Hart's Woods recently, I observed a pattern which has become all too familiar in my nature center consulting work. When the object of a nature center development is to make work for unemployed youth in a community, a Disney World mentality often takes command, and it is the natural attributes which suffer. Some of what I observed suggests that this may be the case in this project. A bird sanctuary that is clear-cut and parklike is more a sanctuary for bird houses and feeders than for birds. A bunny bunker designed to provide winter shelter for rabbits in an area from which all natural winter food sources have been removed is just inviting the rabbits to concentrate on the foundation shrubbery. All natural screening had been removed between sanctuary and schoolyard and between sanctuary and road.

A few years forbearance, of course, would result in the correction of all these inconsistencies, but another, I am sure, has produced a permanent erosion of the wildlife value there. A grapevine, nearly six inches in diameter, was cut and removed because it was an eyesore, or perhaps because it might kill the beech tree host with which it had been coexisting successfully since my youth. Thus is destroyed in seconds a teachable moment that was decades in building.

At least that's the way it seemed to me as I toured those few hallowed acres. I later attempted to reach the project director to discuss these concerns with him, but I was unsuccessful. There may be good reasons for each of these developments that I have criticized. Even if there are not, however, the boyhood pleasures of a departed California forester, and a not-quite-departed environmental educator do not make it hallowed ground to be left untouched. Neither of us have any claim on its future. It should provide sufficient satisfaction that the struggle between nature and civilization still goes on in Hart's Woods. Perhaps an accommodation can be reached there before all that is valuable to nature is removed.

Save That Apple Tree

John Burroughs had a way of conferring poesy on a host of things that many of his contemporaries had never seen as poetic. Witness the transformation that the name wake robin can work on a plant commonly known to the pre-Burroughs world as stinking Benjamin or the similar benefits of substituting trout lily for adder's tongue.

If I possessed a bit of Burroughs's gift, I would like to engender some appreciation for the scrub apple, pear, and thorn bush. The natural fruit produced by these old derelicts doesn't have much value to commerce and evokes mostly curses from homeowners whose lawns they litter. However, to the wild community, from field mouse to deer, they have a golden quality.

Likewise the gnarled trunk and branches, replete with cracks and cavities, are homestead territory for flickers, wrens, downy woodpeckers, or, if we're lucky, bluebirds. Such welcome natives are now often displaced by starling or house sparrow, but those alien invasions cannot be blamed on the apple trees.

Since the apple concentrates on breadth not height in its development, it produces a grand complex of nest sites for robins, waxwings, kingbirds, doves, warblers, and finches. In the densely overgrown apple copse, one may even find at home those lovers of the deeper thicket, the catbird, brown thrasher, or cuckoo. Without

---

Originally published in the *Baldwinsville Messenger*, May 22, 1974; first aired on WRVO-FM, Apr. 13, 1990; published as "Let Us Now Praise Pear, Thorn Bush, Scrub Apple Trees," in the *Herald-Journal*, Apr. 26, 1995 (The Herald Co., Syracuse, NY © Herald-Journal/The Post-Standard. All rights reserved. Reprinted with permission).

straining the imagination too much, we can find benefits bestowed by apples for wildlife in every season, even winter, when deer devour the buds and rabbits and field mice gormandize the bark and twigs.

It is the vernal apple tree that I would like to lionize here. The blooms of cherry, plum, and shad add delightful splashes of white to the otherwise still-drab woodland edge, but the apple, waiting as it does for the first warm spell in May, has a life about it beside which the aforementioned beauties pale. I find much delight in the interplay of colors as those beautiful feathered sprites, the warblers, weave in and out among the branches. Childhood memories of a Blackburnian warbler or an oriole posing prettily in that lovely bower have not been significantly dimmed by the passage of time.

I had a favorite apple tree at the Rogers Center where every spring our dedicated band of birders could share the delight of the warbler–apple blossom combination. The tree bloomed profusely and every year dozens of nosegays were composed by people who found its lowest blossoms irresistible. In summer its branches served

There was an oriole posing prettily in that lovely bower.

the nesting birds. At least a dozen species were seen there during my eight-year tenure. What a lifetime bird list that tree must have had! Youngsters also climbed through those ample boughs. In fall its fruits provided delightful pies and sauces.

Patriarch trees have the advantage over us as witnesses of history. They concentrate on one spot. My Sherburne apple was not older than a man, but it had occupied its spot during just the right span of years. In its developing youth, cheese factory employees enjoyed their lunch breaks in its shade. Later, when the cheese factory was converted to a game farm building, its blossoming corresponded with the first hatches of pheasants each year. It witnessed the crating and shipping of hundreds of thousands of young pheasants over the years.

Next the tree stood passively through the transformation from game farm to conservation education center, and then, just as its golden-age security seemed assured, it was cut to the ground. My successor at the center did not share my satisfaction with age-old apple trees. Its removal was said to be a safety measure, but I remember too well the complaints of the maintenance staff about raking up the apples each year to put too much faith in that explanation. It seems more likely that, despite its annual contribution of bloom and palatable fruit, its career was ended to save a few hours' raking.

I have observed that budget dollars speak much louder than warblers or honey bees. Wild voices are seldom heard without the helpful amplification that a sympathetic human advocate can provide. When the advocate left, so did the tree. To each his own.

If you are the possessor of a golden-aged apple tree, typically gnarled and disreputable, I hope you will consider all these things—its heritage, its hospitality, and its lovely fruitfulness—before you decide it has to go.

The Little Creatures of Autumn

I always greet the turning of the autumn leaves with mixed emotion, for it signifies the winding down of that veritable energy cyclone which is summer in the Northeast. Not that I don't find deep fulfillment in the rich warmth of the fall colors. The flaming reds and oranges of the maples or the shimmering gold of aspen provide a certain very personal kind of high. Still I view the southbound stream of bird life, the dipping angle of the sun, and the constant browning of the meadows with less enthusiasm. At times like these, I often turn my attention to the fall activities of some of nature's little creatures, now more evident because of the rapid disappearance of summer's green curtain.

    I well remember sitting at the gallery window of the Rogers Center at Sherburne one foggy fall morning. I had gone there before dawn to watch the sunrise and to observe the movements of the waterfowl on the marsh. Both were well obscured by the persistent mist, and although my notebook was full of impressions of the marshland sounds, my attention was easily diverted to the nearby feeder. A noisy jay called my attention to the top of an adjacent spruce tree. As I looked up, I was greeted by a memorable and beautiful sight. Every spruce tree was covered from tip to toe by a silken shroud that billowed slightly in the gentle air flow, glistening in the subdued early light. It was as if some giant had acquired the finest silk and carefully wrapped each tree to protect it from the coming blasts of winter.

Originally published in the *Baldwinsville Messenger*, Oct. 18, 1978.

Actually these filmy coverings consisted of thousands of single strands spun by balloon spiders, which perform a ritual migration each fall. They climb to the highest available point and launch into the air to drift before the gentle breeze at the end of a silken tether. By themselves the slender strands are barely visible, but when covered with dew or frost and accompanied by thousands of their kind they produce spectacular results. It is a good lesson on the cumulative effects of the small efforts of tiny creatures. The balloon spider is not much more than one-twentieth of an inch in length, but its numbers are so great that they represent a significant presence when made visible by the dew or fog.

Another little creature whose work I admire is the funnel-web grass spider. It is present in the grass throughout the growing season, but I only think to look for it in late summer or early fall. Just a few weeks ago, I was enjoying an early morning walk. It was a day when the pumpkins were turning and the delicate heads of witches' grass were beginning to provide a silvery frame for the pumpkin patch. The mist had polished the witches' grass to a high gloss, and I was too busy admiring it as I traversed a plot of orchard grass to notice that my feet were becoming very wet. I looked down and beheld the presence of an almost continuous gossamer carpet connecting the bases of the grass clumps. The carpet was made up of hundreds of the diaphanous horizontal webs of the grass spider, each replete with a funnel descending to the ground where the spider rested. The carpet was so thin that I had ripped it asunder wherever I had walked, displacing the few spiders that still remained.

What brings this all to mind is the recent solution, I think, of a longtime mystery that involves one of my paintings. I paint to share with others visual delights or biological secrets I have discovered. A few years ago, on a bright autumn afternoon, I was strolling down a lane between hedgerow and corn field when I noticed several chickadees moving back and forth between the browning corn and the hedge. One landed on a broken-down, partly browned cornstalk, coming to rest above an ear from which the husk had been partly removed. I was quite taken with the scene and decided it would make

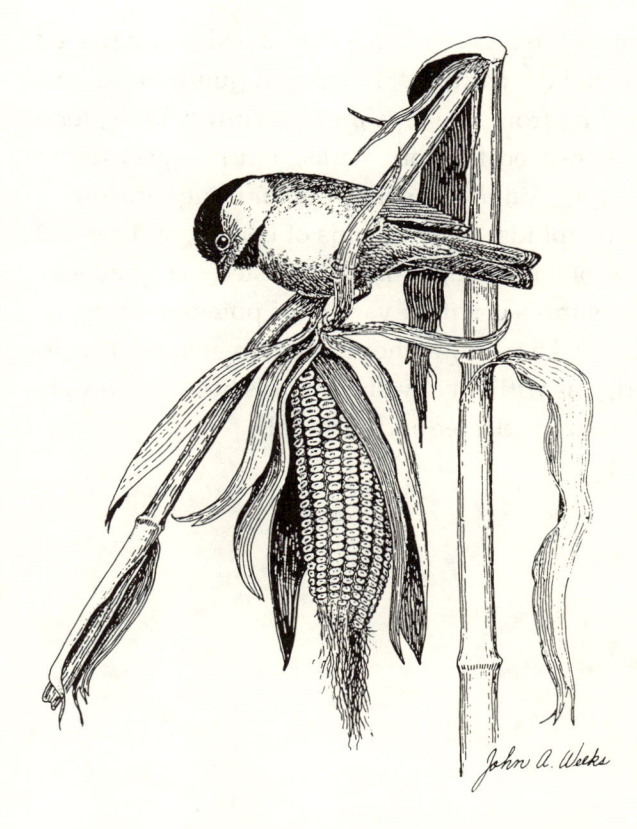

A chickadee landed on a broken-down, partly browned cornstalk.

a good painting. Realizing that the chickadee was not after the corn, I began an unsuccessful search for the object of its interest.

Some time later I executed the painting, a combination of ochres and subdued green in which the white face of the chickadee and the yellow corn stand out. It turned out to be a popular painting. A few knowledgeable birders have commented that some insect, egg mass, or spider should be added to counteract the impression that the chickadee is after the corn. Each time I have renewed my effort to define a suitable target for the chickadee, I always end up leaving the painting as it is. After all, I did see the chickadee in the corn and was not able to identify its objective, so the painting is an honest sharing of a nature experience that remains a mystery.

The issue arose again when it was decided to use the design for an art print for Centers for Nature Education. Again I went to the corn fields to seek an answer. As I emerged from a hedge and turned into the lane that skirted the cornfield, I observed hundreds of gossamer threads extending from tree tops into the corn field. Balloon spiders ballooning. I checked the corn stalks, and though I found none of the tiny spiders, I did observe many other things, including forlorn little broods of aphids, several kinds of beetles, and several kinds of flies, any one of which might have interested a chickadee.

Now I have been supplied with a variety of potential answers, but lacking a chickadee, I am still without a certain answer. The art print, when finished, was without any of autumn's little creatures to divert our attention from chickadee and corn stalk.

Alien Invaders

One of the great environmental experiments that helped to ring in the twentieth century was the introduction of foreign wildlife into American coverts that had been extensively changed by the agricultural and industrial revolutions.

The premise seems to have been that native wildlife was on the wane and a shot in the arm from foreign fields was just what was needed. There was a certain undeniable logic in all this, if you equate sociological and ecological premises. After all, America was the global melting pot. It had taken the best from every land and forged that varied best into a new sociological amalgam. If it worked for people, certainly it would work for wildlife.

Therefore hart and hind from Europe and Asia were imported including the red deer, the fallow, and the sika deer. At best the success was modest. A good thing, really, for the most magnificent of all the deer clan, the eastern white tail, seemingly extirpated from farm country, was planning a resurgence. Sika or fallow deer, for all their beauty, would have been poor substitutes had they succeeded.

Then there were the birds, mostly game birds. The black cock, the capercaillie, the red grouse, the Hungarian partridge, and the gray quail were introduced to provide hunting opportunity. With some notable exceptions, these birds, too, proved most unwilling to set up housekeeping in America. Many just disappeared. Some prospered briefly and then dispersed without further issue.

Most successful of those turn-of-the-century introductions were the house sparrow (English sparrow to the older generation) and the

First aired on WRVO-FM, June 2, 1989.

30 | **Remembering**

European starling. Both have proved at best a mixed blessing, and the starling, the most abundant of birds in America, has reputedly displaced more than one native species.

Of all the introduced birds, the most welcome, without doubt, has been the ring-necked pheasant. I've shared my admiration for this dapper dandy many times, for this fine bird has both the lines and the lifestyle of which legends are made. For a non-native, the pheasant has few detractors. People and wildlife, however, are not equal in any eyes lower than those of the creator, and approval by people is no assurance of success in the wild.

The pheasant was established in Central New York coverts by a decades-long blitz of game-farm-reared birds. It's an interesting conundrum that most studies have shown a remarkably poor survival from those ten- to fifteen-week-old chicks customarily released during the heyday of the game farm operation. That statistic notwithstanding, the pheasant followed the flow and prospered in good farmland reaching a maximum population, I believe, during the 1940s.

During the 1950s as a practicing wildlife biologist, I had a low re-

The pheasant has both the lines and the lifestyle of which legends are made.

gard for the efficacy of pheasant propagation and release. Natural pheasant reproduction appeared adequate. Still I can imagine my old mentor, Dick Reynolds, one of the brightest and best men I ever knew, saying, "Well, Weeksie, you'll notice how pheasant populations dwindled right along with the phasing out of the game farm program." That coincidence might be hard to explain away.

It's important to realize, too, that the ring-neck of New York State is indeed a game farm production, not wholly an Asian and not identical with any indigenous native bird. The records show that the New York bird was of mixed parentage, mostly Eastern Chinese ringneck, a bird of the agricultural areas of China, but also part Mongolian and part Caucasian blackneck. The Mongolian bird was supposed to add color and the ability to withstand severe winter weather. The blackneck was said to possess a unique wildness. How scientific this all was is debatable, I guess, but our bird is more colorful than the paler Eastern Chinese ringneck and it did appear to winter well, at least during its heyday.

It's wildness was more debatable. Many sportsmen have always complained that the game-farm-released birds were real patsies. Too tame! They wouldn't stand to the dog and wouldn't flush. My limited research indicated the opposite. In those few years when we had a chance to liberate adult game farm birds just before or during the hunting season, success measured in birds bagged per hour of hunting was best. It was the wild-reared birds that were best at escaping the gun.

All of this last commentary may seem less than edifying to those who are unaware of my career as a wildlife biologist and game manager. Hunting opportunity was once my business. Since hunting opportunity was never a high priority for me, I eventually moved on to a longer career in environmental education. However, I learned a great deal the first seven years after my graduation from Cornell, and one of the principal outcomes was an understanding and respect for all people interested in the out-of-doors. Often the sportsman's perspective was far more sound than those of the preservationist.

The pheasant was an important ambassador in all of this. Since it was raised and liberated for hunting, using funds provided by hunters, it was seldom the center of acrimony between the hunter and the non-hunter, and like deer and rabbit, its numbers were determiners of, not resulting from, hunting pressure. At any rate I am heartened by the modest resurgence of the pheasant locally. May its tribe increase.

Half Steps in History

In 1992 we celebrated the 500th anniversary of Columbus's first footfall in the new world. It was a fateful event. Thinking about that I've often wondered if Columbus left any discernable footprints behind him, and if so, did any native who found them recognize their implications? Certainly Columbus's effect on the new world was minimal, and yet the very fact of his discovery produced a reaction that in time would make a permanent change on the whole continent.

If we move forward in time half the distance between Columbus's time and today, 250 years, we arrive at 1742. Most of North America still seemed untouched by Europe's invasion, except perhaps for the colonies along the East Coast. There the signs of things to come would be evident. There the forests were being cleared for agriculture. Boston was a developing metropolis, New York City a burgeoning village and Washington, D.C., yet to be even envisioned.

Another half step forward is 125 years and would put us in 1867, just two years before the Atlantic and Pacific coasts would be linked by rail. It was the year of the Reconstruction Act. There were thirty-two states and seven territories, and although the frontier was not quite gone, nearly eighty percent of the population lived outside the cities. New England hill farmers had already seen the effect of overly intensive use of the land and many had moved on to similar acreages in New York and Pennsylvania. There would be one more cycle of overuse and abandonment before the people would be resettled by the government.

First aired on WRVO-FM, May 2, 1986.

34 | Remembering

Although agricultural land use was approaching its maximum, with more land in cultivation than ever before or since, there was more of the frontier than of civilization in the aspect of the land. Few people worried about the extinction of plants or animals. The passenger pigeon still migrated in the billions. The bear, wolf, and bison had disappeared from the landscape and were largely unlamented since every one of them competed with the preferred land use of the day, agriculture.

The next half-step forward would be sixty-two and one half years and would place us in mid-1929. What a fateful time both for people and environment. The bottom was due to fall out of many people's well-laid plans including what had seemed for its time an unprecedented assault on the natural environment. The well-oiled machinery of economic development was producing an escalating exodus from the land into the city, which, by all accounts, was the finest of places to live.

On the land another time-honored institution, farming as a way

Bear, wolf, and bison had disappeared from the landscape.

of life as opposed to a business, was given a boost by the Depression. We are told that no one needed starve on the farm, but within a few short years those people with ancestral roots in the New England hill country who had resettled in similar New York countryside found that this land, too, had limited durability as a site for farming. By the time of the crash, the land had pretty well played out, as it had throughout the Appalachian Highlands.

As a part of its massive program of economic relief, the government proposed to remove these subsistence farmers from their marginal land to better situations. Though many were reluctant to be uprooted, they had no choice, and the federal government became the custodian of many impoverished acres. Some of the land was redistributed to the states, but much of it remained under direct federal landlordship. It became the backbone of a state and national park movement and management area program from which we still, as nature enthusiasts, reap many benefits. The Happy Valley and Little John Wildlife Management Areas in Oswego and Lewis counties, and the Pharsalia and Tioughnioga areas in Chenango and Madison counties are remnants of that effort.

The decade of the thirties would see the initiation of many other programs designed specifically to maintain the quality and productivity of the land itself. Such agencies and programs as the Soil Conservation Service, Agricultural Conservation and Stabilization, Civilian Conservation Corps, and the federal Fish and Wildlife Service were founded. There is much more to the story than this. Suffice to say that the conservation programs of the thirties produced an understanding of and an ethic about resource conservation that still resounds in segments of the populace.

The next half step forward spans thirty-one years and brings us into the 1960s, a decade whose ramifications are still being studied. Environmentally we might usher it in with Rachel Carson's *Silent Spring* and out with the first Earth Day on college campuses. It was an era of increasing environmental awareness. It was also a time of emerging third world countries, many of whom would soon be claiming the right to exploit their resources as we had ours in an earlier era. Many of us opposed their land use techniques then and still do now, but lacking a global resource ethic we have neither legal nor moral status.

The next half leap of fifteen and a half years to 1976 is a point where the environmental passion had begun to wane for many and global resource development escalated. For the first time, some of us took a hard look at vanishing species of plants and animals with an attempt to classify and engender some public awareness. We also began to see the positive effects of conservation as we attempted to husband our fuel.

The next half step is only seven years and it brings us into the 1980s, an era when we can envision the disappearance of rain forests and begin to assign possible life spans to whale species.

You can continue that half step game indefinitely and never reach your goal. It is significant, though, that today with computers and nearly 500 years of experience, we can recognize and measure the impact of our footfalls. What we are finding is that the dynamics of population shift and economic development are such that the capacity of the environment to absorb these footfalls is beginning to dwindle.

After 500 years of change, we've reached the point where foresight needs to replace hindsight in our celebrations.

Opening Day and Buck Fever

It's six o'clock of a November morning as I step from my door. The stars are brilliant and the air brisk. The handle of the Big Dipper is pointing eastward and Orion is stalking the western sky near the horizon. There is just a hint of dawning over the eastern hills. I start my car and head toward a favorite restaurant, watching the rapid spread of dawn's early light. As it encompasses the vault of the heavens, it silhouettes a few dark stratus clouds just above the earth. Otherwise the sky is quite clear. By the time I reach the restaurant about seven miles away, it is so bright that I can no longer distinguish Cassiopeia's lazy W.

The restaurant is crowded with brightly clothed or camouflaged men, whose demeanor and nervous energy identify them as if they bore signs reading, "I am a deer hunter." It is the opening day of deer season, and the hunters have less than an hour to find a promising spot, so they don't linger long after my arrival. Too bad. I love to listen to their accounts of the hunt, the hunted, and the special techniques that allow them to get their quarry.

Don't misunderstand. I am not sanguine about the kill, but then neither are these Nimrods. They are much less the brutish inhumane souls than many who hate the thought of hunting would have you believe. My ambivalence is annoying to them, too, but I defend it simply on the basis of nearly sixty years of experience since I first

Originally published in the *Norwich Evening Sun*, Nov. 26, 1966. First aired on WRVO-FM, Dec. 1, 1989.

came to question the hunt, including a decade when the deer season was part of my job each year.

I choose a well-lit booth next to a sextet of brightly clad seniors whose passion for the hunt seems somewhat blunted by the years. What, I wonder, will these men have to say about the annual search for antlers? Eavesdropping proves that the present conversation is mostly about operations of the kind that are common to men of our age, including what they can and can no longer attempt, and what prescriptions are required to keep them going.

It is some time before the conversation turns to the hunt. At first it is almost a debate about whether or not they are actually even going to consummate this planned outing. Finally, they get down to business, each revealing his intentions for watch or for sortie. There is a certain aspect of ritual in all this. The plan has been followed, one would suspect for years, slightly modified from time to time to reflect past success and failure.

About ten minutes before the season is due to open, they get up almost reluctantly to take their stands in nearby copses and hedgerows, perhaps even in the concealment of a patch of still standing corn. The atmosphere is heavy with nostalgia. For them this is just one more, perhaps one last, attempt to recall the special celebrations of their youth, that aspect of the hunt that no non-hunter can understand or abide. We are the products of our life experiences, and we are programmed or patterned by the values that surrounded them. This is often the point at which the hunter and the non-hunter find their fundamental misunderstandings.

As for myself, the opening day of the deer season brings back a host of memories dating back to my first dawning interest in nature. I grew up in a hunting family, one where the lore included only a peripheral interest in deer. The deer had not yet reclaimed Orleans County's woodlots and draws. I remember well the first deer to appear on our farm. On that occasion we forgot the constrictions of the Depression, the domestic and foreign policy concerns revealed by Franklin D. Roosevelt's fireside chats, to celebrate this event of nature.

I remember well the first deer to appear on our farm.

It wasn't many years later that the first antlerless deer season opened in the Southern Tier, and we motored southward to share in the hunt with friends, nearly as close as relatives, who lived in Steuben County. My cousin Doug was thoroughly disgusted with me because I chose to watch rather than shoot when a gangly male fawn, fair game, passed within twenty yards of me. His father and my brothers passed it off as buck fever, and Doug instantly forgave me my lapse.

Actually, it wasn't buck fever at all. It was just the opposite. It was my first opportunity to observe a deer up close, and I needed to imbibe and to write the experience indelibly on my heart and in my memory banks. It took years before my family understood, probably better than I did at the time, why I was such a poor, even reluctant, marksman.

As with the seniors in the next booth who prepared for the hunt by discussing operations and heating systems, the hunt became ritual and my attention was drawn more to the magnificence of the quarry and to the reactions of my companions than it was to any thought of the kill.

Observing Spring

The rain has come
  with thunder clashing
  falling to the earth,
    pelting the ground
    creating streams
  wetting all unprotected to the bone

And after
  all is hushed: a strange
  feeling hovers over the earth
    the air is fresh, clean
    fragrant
  the earth seems new—
Ah, the rain — JWD

By many standards, spring is the most spectacular season of the year. It is like a great reciprocating engine that has been idle for months. When first fired, using fuel that has been in the tank through the winter, it sputters, misfires, and finally catches. Every Central New Yorker knows that spring will not run smoothly until the sun has mounted and the engine is fully warmed up.

Still, spring is the most colorful and vivacious of the seasons, in part because it starts out in such a barren state, brown and uninviting. Each new addition to the early spring commentary is a spectacular breath of fresh air, the more effective because of its drab setting.

I know botanists and ecologists who fault the astronomers for declaring spring at the equinox. "Too early," they say. Spring starts for them with the first emergence of new plant life a month later. In evaluating this controversy over when spring begins, it is important to remember that every bit of the early spring community is a gift from the previous seasons. Only the sunlight itself is new, and it can be used only after seeds or buds have sprouted using stored energy. Even the first new births are the products of gestations initiated during the winter.

By the time the engine is operating smoothly, however, sometime following May Day, there is a flood of new life and new growth. Spring has indeed sprung and it has just over a month, according to the calendar, to develop its full potential. Again the botanist demurs. As soon as the leaves are fully erupted, the plant lover is ready to declare summer.

The best frame of mind with which to observe spring is to see it as nature's sunrise, a brief but explosive period between the dark of winter and the full light of summer.

April Sunshine

I've said it before. There's something special about April sunshine. It's nothing I can tell by my inexpert analysis of the nature of the light itself. Admittedly it does look different to me, but that doesn't really mean too much. Everything looks different to me in April. That's more reflection than observation.

It's what the sun produces that shows me the difference. April sun calls forth the first shoots of hepatica, coaxing open its first shy blooms. April sun also proliferates the pale golden blooms of coltsfoot, which hesitantly ventured forth while March still held sway. Then in proper sequence come cohosh, which is hardly noticed, the small but lovely spring beauty, and the showy but fleeting bloodroot. By the end of April, the cumulative effect of the April sun has produced an almost bewildering array of green shoots and swollen buds.

May's colorful woodland carpet is a direct legacy from April sunshine. The old saw "April showers bring May flowers" is too incomplete for me. Even the April showers themselves are a product of the mounting sun.

Plants are pivotal in determining the course of animal activities, but again it is April's special light that produces the comely interplay of birds and mammals as well as the primordial stirrings of the amphibians. The swelling chorus of wood frog, peeper, leopard frog, and toad is an April symphony orchestrated by the sun.

Of course, I will admit that all of these April–May events we celebrate are cumulative. All of April's passion plays, be it bird

First aired on WRVO-FM, Apr. 9, 1993.

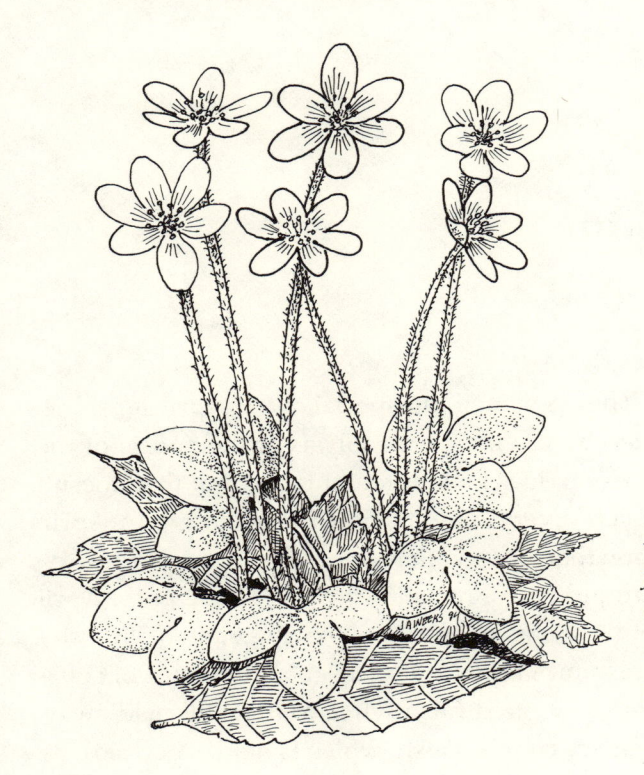

April sun calls forth the first shoots of hepatica, coaxing open its first shy blooms.

courtship, mammalian birthing, or the great convocation of the amphibians, have been well rehearsed. They use scripts that are entirely internal, involving the flow of hormones and the development of reproductive capacities.

April's baby cottontails were initiated in March, and the first pale blue eggs of the bluebird can be traced without too much extrapolation back to the winter solstice. After all, fruitful bluebird nesting has to be preceded each year by the maturation of the gonads, migration, courtship, pair selection, and breeding. Without a moment's hesitation, nest site selection, egg laying, incubation, and intensive feeding all have to be accomplished before balmy May can receive its first infusion of new bluebirds.

It's a lengthy scenario that requires much more than one lunar cycle to run its course, but April, you see, is when it all becomes real to us. A single devoted male bluebird reflecting the early morning April sunshine is the trigger that allows us to join in the procession.

I know that there are those who are put off by the intensity of my emotional involvement with this festival. I'm not going to apologize for my joyful response. There aren't too many ways in which I can pass on to others the essence of my mother's deep response to her creator's gifts. Like David of old, she saw it all as glorious. My good fortune is that she handed those perceptions on to me. I'm sure that she intended me to nourish and embellish them and never to withhold them.

It's not necessary, however, to fantasize and embellish April's gifts to find them impressive. April's arithmetic is itself staggering. I know of an April wetland that is virtually nothing throughout the rest of the year. April is its recital time. Ordinarily it is a one-acre, six-inch-deep swale, but in April it swells to nearly ten acres, a temporary accumulation of over three million gallons of water daily, the excess of its inflow over its outflow. Its watershed is approximately one-two hundred fiftieth the area of Onondaga County, and every square inch of Onondaga County feeds into one watershed or another.

What a grand surplus of water we see each spring. Too bad that we've worked so hard to get rid of it as fast as we can, resulting sometimes in flooded fields, roadways, even homes and places of business. This results directly from two miscalculations made by those who insist there should be no restrictions on their exploitation of their land. One is the filling of wetlands, which had in their natural state served as flood-preventing pressure valves for maverick watersheds. The other is insisting on occupying flood plains, which have had a history of periodic flooding from primeval times.

We could sum it all up by saying that no one bothers to calculate the astronomical amount of water that blesses our land each year and so we are completely unprepared to receive this gift.

We could also find impressive numbers in the migrants passing over and through our woods and wetland on their way north. I don't have any estimates, but they do constitute, as Aldo Leopold has reminded us, a living wind. I wonder what we would understand if we could count the number of wing beats represented by this living wind.

Well, enough of paeans to April. It doesn't need my poor efforts. April is indeed a superlative biotic symphony.

The Springtime Juggernaut

I'm constantly amazed by the escalating energy of spring. It is like a mushroom that lingers in its rootlike mycelia just beneath the surface of the ground and then suddenly bursts forth to reach its full form almost overnight. Spring is a whole wagonload of mushrooms bursting on the land.

A single seed smaller than a caraway seed can produce a giant ragweed that resembles a small tree. A small clutch of eggs in the bottom of a grass and fiber cradle can produce a nest full of appetites within a month of the egg's first formation. Insects have to produce similar miracles to be available in sufficient numbers to satisfy the appetites of the birds and maintain their own populations.

Many people don't believe this could just happen. They find it

First aired on WRVO-FM, May 6, 1994.

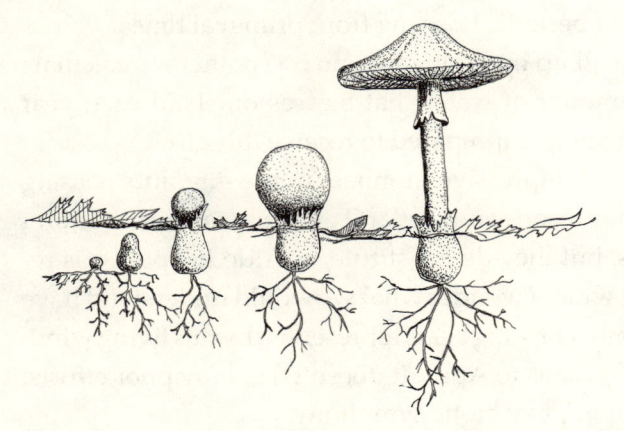

Spring is a whole wagonload of mushrooms.

difficult to understand how this could all be so neatly orchestrated without a great director setting the tempo. Part of our inability to comprehend is due to the fact that we presume the pace of spring has to be orderly with specific goals and products. It does follow rules, but they are very general and they never really define what the ultimate product should be.

When I was studying aquatic biology, we were introduced to the concept of productivity per cubic foot. Many of you who own aquaria may actually use it as a rule of thumb. It says that any cubic foot of water—depending on temperature, nutrients, gasses, and other things—will support a certain total mass of life. The pond doesn't care, according to the rule, how this mass is put together. It could be in the classic example, ten one-inch fish or one ten-inch fish. It is a useful idea, but it's not very accurate. It doesn't distinguish between fish. In a real pond it makes a difference, for instance, how many of the fish are plant eaters and how many are animal eaters.

Still, to those who understand the rule's limitations, it can be helpful. The same kind of rule can be applied to upland communities, too. What really determines the nature and complexity of that burgeoning spring landscape is its capacity to convert sunlight to usable energy. Its capacity is great, but there are, indeed, limits. The fact that a song sparrow or cecropia moth fails or succeeds may have nothing to do with its species but may depend on its position in the energy chain. If its job is already filled, it may not survive there.

Late fall and winter are usually the periods when these survival decisions are made. We call the judgments starvation or exposure or predation. They help to maintain the needed energy balance. It's kind of a depressing idea, and I confess that a part of my enjoyment of spring erupting on the land is that it practically wipes out the necessity for the juries to meet and for judgments to be delivered.

Spring is consistently bountiful, and even though its lavishness may necessitate survival judgments later on, for now spring is just nature showing off. Right now I know of a place where eight tiny rabbits are preparing to flee the nest. They'll find lots of company when they do. Rabbits do not demand large homesteads. Neither do some birds. Last year, while painting a picture of a brown thrasher and crab apple blossoms, I found two nests. One held four or five nestling cardinals. The other would harbor within a week a clutch of sky blue catbird eggs. I was able to observe that both nests produced fledgling young and that both were joined in the same hedgerow by subsequent nests of warblers and goldfinches.

The survival judgment panel delivered no decisions during this time, but some young birds did die for various reasons. None of those had anything to do with energy budget. Still, the elements of next year's garden cast of characters begin to line up. By fall the slate will be complete, and its final nature will be declared by the judgment panel through the winter.

While I have been thus woolgathering, a house wren has delivered the first wren carol of the year. I am pleased to know that at least one male wren has escaped winter judgment. Later on the same day, swamp sparrow and least flycatcher sign in. Off the late flight, perhaps. By late afternoon my list of new arrivals has reached a dozen, and the nature of this year's extravaganza is beginning to emerge.

It now awaits the confirmation that these are, indeed, our own and that they will occupy traditional sites with traditional vigor. Someday soon, the brilliant come-hither call of the thrasher will beckon me to begin the annual census, telling me what I want to know about the prospects for next year.

Meanwhile, nature's judgment panel is on vacation, or at least reclining in a neutral corner. Good thing. This is the time for joyous greeting, not farewell.

Watching the Geese at Vann Road

It is at this moment of each year that I wish I were a muskrat, eye-deep in the marsh. —ALDO LEOPOLD

The joys of nature are not restricted to those who rise early, dress appropriately, and hike much. Some of my best natural history lessons have been monitored through the kitchen window, while dressed for church, or while still dressed for bed. The only essential ingredient is desire to experience. Herewith, I recount one of those great moments viewed entirely from the driver's seat of my car.

The sun is not yet up, but the sky at the horizon is beginning to show a warm red glow as I hurry from the house to my car. The thermometer registers 32 degrees, but it actually feels colder. It is just 4:45 A.M. as I head my car in the direction of Beaver Lake. Even at this distance, I can hear that the geese are expectantly awaiting my arrival. After all, it is an annual ritual we share.

I pull in to the Vann Road overlook at 4:50 A.M.. The lake is uniformly covered with geese. I don't attempt to count the many thousands but just concentrate on the beauty of their graceful silhouettes against the warmly tinted water. They draw back briefly from the shoreline but slowly drift in again. There is a car already there, but no passengers in sight. I will be joined by several others as the morning progresses.

I get out my notebook, open the window, and pour a cup of coffee from my thermos. I note a few geese in the sky already. As one par-

Originally published in the *Baldwinsville Messenger*, Apr. 20, 1977.

ticularly vocal flock passes overhead, the chorus on the lake swells to double volume. The geese seem nervous and expectant.

At 4:58, the first flight of three geese leaves the lake, passing directly overhead. The lakeside peanut gallery sends them off with a rousing cheer, or perhaps a warning. I'm never quite sure about goose talk. The early risers continue to leave in groups of twos and threes. The chorus swells and diminishes with each departure.

At 5:10, with the sun still hidden behind the horizon, the first real flight of seven leaves. These first excursions are probably family affairs. It seems that with geese, too, some families have a penchant for early arrival. I watch the nuances of color reflected by the gently stirring water: rose, pearl, pink, and copper, a gentle reflection of the rapidly brightening skyline.

At 5:15, a flock of about a dozen leaves. They take off in a southeasterly direction but then double back for one more vocal salute to the resting multitudes. The response is deafening. I notice a hint of mist, hanging like gossamer cobwebs over the water, slowly drifting eastward before a gentle breeze. Some of the watchers get out of their cars. The geese drift back from the shoreline again. A red-winged blackbird lifts his voice above the chorus.

At 5:20 A.M., the skyline is visibly lightening and losing its rosy hue. A few ducks take off, followed at 5:22 by about 150 geese. They pass right overhead, flying low. I hear the first comment, "Incredible," from the human gallery. The chorus lifts again as another 250 geese rise up in front of us and set off in purposeful fashion toward town. The sun is poking above the horizon as a dozen more flocks take off. Their breasts glow in the sunlight, and as they move southward they are etched against the still purple cloud bases.

At 5:35, a mass exodus fills the sky with sinuous lines and partly formed Vs. The population on the lake is thinning noticeably.

By 5:45, when the waters begin to reflect the blue sky and the remaining mist glows in the first sunlight, there are more geese in the air than on the lake. The horizons are liberally laced with lines of geese. The pattern is indeed incredible. Within ten minutes, the rooftops in Plainville and Baldwinsville will resound to their foraging calls, and soon after the grain fields will receive them.

Watching the Geese at Vann Road | 51

Within ten minutes, the rooftops of Plainville and Baldwinsville will resound to the geese's foraging calls.

By 5:55, the aerial pageant has run its course; the few remaining geese on the lake seem reluctant to leave at all. A few stragglers are casting about and calling loudly in search of companions. I decide it is time for me to do the same, and set off for home and an early breakfast.

The Courtship of Amphibians

One thing I never tire of talking about is the annual observance of courtship in nature, the process by which mates are wooed and won and the necessary replenishment of kind is assured.

A certain fascination with this process is natural, I think. Young wildlife has a nearly universal appeal even to those who can't quite deal with any other aspect of wild nature. People sometimes value young creatures more highly than their natural parents do. Instinct may cause an animal to abandon the weak or malformed offspring, the very individual on whom the human animal lover will lavish the most attention.

That, too, is understandable enough when analyzed, but it's not that facet of the reproductive cycle I'm referring to here. There is an equally comely set of happenings that precedes the production of offspring that few people really appreciate. Known to many is the strange and colorful courtship flight of the woodcock, the drumming of the ruffed grouse, the posturing and sparring of pheasants. Just as interesting but less well known is the strange behavior of frogs, toads, salamanders, even turtles and fish.

Let's venture forth on the first evening when the night temperatures approach 50°F. Our destination is a low-lying streamside swale, and our approach is heralded by a chorus of surprising sounds, perhaps the ducklike quacks of the wood frog, the tinkling chorus of spring peepers, or the high-pitched trill of toads. I'm sure

First aired on WRVO-FM, Apr. 1, 1988.

you've all heard those things even if you weren't aware of the identity of the callers. A few people, I know, have even called it an infernal racket. That's not the way these hopping amphibians view it.

First, the chorus itself is a great attraction to individuals emerging from winter hibernation. The vocalization is frequently referred to as a rallying call. We have to believe, too, that it's more than that, perhaps even a declaration of reproductive sufficiency. Another way to look at it is that it might also be a conditioner, even an arouser of long-sleeping instinct.

Whatever its purpose, the calling individuals congregate, and from there they act as individuals, seeking out the proper sharer of this god-given proclivity. We tend to suspect that the selectivity is not well defined, even hit or miss, but we don't really know. Each species has its own special ritual, partly vocal, partly behavioral, and the result is the production of several hundred, even thousands, of eggs per individual along with the proper supply of sperm-containing milt to fertilize a high percentage of the eggs.

What happens next varies somewhat with the species. For toads or leopard frogs, the proliferation of cells and the final definition of a new individual is so rapid that you can almost see it occurring before you. Within a week or ten days, those gelatinous globs of BB-sized eggs will have developed into fishlike miniatures perhaps a half-inch long that we call tadpoles.

Theirs is a hazardous life. To many of their animal neighbors, they look like food. Very few of the thousands upon thousands of those that hatch in each little wet hole will live to voice their rallying call another spring. But that's part of the genius of the system. Even with the high mortality rate, we don't lack for frogs or toads. The productivity is very high.

The rallying and reproductive patterns are partly responsible for that, as is the mode of reproduction itself. It's a shotgun pattern: strew out hundreds or thousands of eggs, bathe them in milt, and then let nature take its course. Quite different from deer or Canada goose, which zealously nourish and accompany their few offspring for many months. This is not to suggest, either, that no amphibians care for or guard their offspring. Some do, and they are rewarded with better survival for it.

The pattern is there, however, and it is interesting to observe. Don boots, take a good flashlight, and travel after sundown to one of the local roadside wet holes from which clacking, grunting, trilling, or ba-rooming is emanating. Approach quietly and once there, stay still until the chorus, temporarily silenced by your approach, resumes. Then carefully play your flashlight over the water and vegetation.

Thumbnail-sized peepers, larger toads, and wood frogs shine with a pale glow in the artificial light. Leopard frogs, green frogs, and bullfrogs are large enough to be easily spotted once you are accustomed to looking for them. Now the important thing is to watch what they are doing. If the light is not too overpowering, most of the species will continue their activities. I guarantee you'll find it interesting.

Spring Thunder and a Native American

The list of living native Americans grows shorter with each passing decade, perhaps because the native land itself is fast disappearing. The ruffed grouse is such a native, one of the few that have remained unchanged by the pressure of a human-dominated environment.

On the vast stage of primeval America, the grouse was and remains today an actor in the grand manner of the past. Observe him for a moment. His platform is an old log, partly covered with moss. He starts with his back toward us, tail feathers spread fanlike, and ruff feathers raised in a circle around his neck. He makes one or two tentative silent wing beats, then, setting his tail back on the log, he begins to stroke in earnest. They are strange, almost horizontal strokes, accompanied by a thump of peculiar resonance. Although the beats are slow and measured at first, the tempo increases rapidly, ending in a muffled roll not unlike distant thunder.

Analysis by motion picture has shown that each performance requires about eight seconds, start to finish, and that the sound is definitely made by the wings striking the air in a forward and upward motion. The drumming may be repeated immediately or it may be accompanied by a strutting display that rivals the drumming in dignity and impressiveness. During this display, the male raises his tail in a vertical fanlike semicircle, lowers his wings until they almost drag on the ground, pulls back his head and erects his ruff until it forms a deep brown collar. He struts back and forth like a miniature tom turkey, hissing and pecking and rapidly gyrating his head.

Originally published in the *Baldwinsville Messenger*, Apr. 17, 1975; first aired on WRVO-FM, Apr. 27, 1990.

56 | Observing Spring

The grouse starts with his back toward us, tail feathers spread fanlike and ruff feathers raised.

The performance may be repeated throughout the year, but it is most frequent and most meaningful in the spring when it is associated with the establishment of territory and the breeding season. The performance is initiated similarly in front of either rival male or member of the harem; however, the similarity ends at the point when the spectator identifies itself as male or female.

Once mating occurs, the female seeks a secluded spot, usually at the base of a tree, bush, log, or stone in the open woods. Here a slight depression is created in the forest floor, and nine to fourteen lightly splotched buff-colored eggs are laid. After twenty-three or twenty-four days the eggs hatch, and the downy young are able to run about and search for food soon after they dry off. The hen convoys them about, constantly talking to her foraging young with reassuring clucks. The chicks appear well disciplined and will remain still and silent, even when nearly stepped upon. The chicks grow rapidly and are soon able to fly weakly for short distances. By fall, they are full grown. The brood may remain together into the fall, and when flushed together provide quite a thrill.

The ruffed grouse is seasonal in its cover choices, following a pattern of food and cover needs. In fall, it tends to inhabit the hedgerows, shrub fields, overgrown orchards, and pioneer woodlands where fruits and weed seeds abound. In winter, the grouse seeks out the mixed woodlots where hemlock or spruce provide shelter and fresh hardwood buds provide nourishment. In spring, the birds move to the more mature woodlands in search of drumming logs and nest sites. By summer, the birds begin to search for shrubbery and herbaceous fields where insects abound for the fresh hatched chicks and a variety of seeds and succulent foliage exists for the fledglings.

Most of this information escapes the hunter whose only exposure to grouse is found in the company of dog and shotgun, and consists of the explosive flutter of wings and the glimpse of an elusive jet-propelled bundle of feathers, seeking to put screening cover between itself and its pursuer with the utmost dispatch.

It may be that no other native bird has so many comely features, so romantic a reputation, and such steadfast fondness for overgrown land. The grouse seems to find it impossible to adjust to intensive agriculture, and its numbers wax and wane with the land-use cycles. It finds its best prosperity in times and places where the human economy is least bullish. It can persist in this country only so long as mature mixed woodlots and shrub-grown fields remain.

A Word in Defense of the Dandelion

Just the other day I heard an announcement from the National Lawn Institute—I think that's the organization—pointing out the dire implications of the fact that in my lawn there are too many weeds per square inch and not enough blades of grass. Their optimum was, I believe, six grass plants per square foot. That's dozens of blades. I don't know how they heard about my lawn, and I don't know who was counting the number of grass stems per square foot to find out that mine is deficient. They needn't have invested the time; I could have told them.

My lawn, you see, is a work of art, created by a studied unconcern about the number of weed seeds per square inch. Some of my neighbors might characterize my lawn-care method as neglect. Not so. My younger son, who still lives at home, mows the lawn with assiduous regularity. No one in our neighborhood has a better record of mowings per season. What's the difference, then? Simple.

When I contemplate the number of weed seeds in my lawn, I rejoice, hoping fervently that among the 4,704,000 seeds will be a smattering of heavenly blue veronica, some common plantain, a bit of orange hawkweed, a goodly measure of fragrant purple violet, some Dutch clover, and, yes, even a sprinkling of golden dandelion. I'll admit that my lawn lacks somewhat in its representation of the red spectrum. In droughty seasons when other lawns are uniform brown, like curing hay, my lawn has annoying patches of bright green supplied by the succulent weeds whose broad green leaves are

First aired on WRVO-FM, May 1, 1987.

immune to desiccation. It's exactly that feature of my lawn I admire most.

See, I have to tell you right out that the uniform green sward indicated by six plants of grass per square foot is just plain boring to me. It's boring as a concept and as an entity. It's not that it's green. I love green, every shade of green you can think of. In fact, I adore seeing them intermixed as they are in anything that's natural.

Do you constantly assault your lawn with chemicals and sharp instruments? Do you judge your success by the uniform greenness of the grass? I don't! To me, that uniform green rectangle is as devoid of creativity as is a piece of green construction paper, framed and supplied with a mystic title, hanging in a major gallery.

I know my bourgeois roots are showing. The paintings I admire are those in which the artist has expertly swatched the pigments on the palette allowing them to intermix spontaneously. Then, even more expertly, that artist has dipped a brush in the olio and deftly applied it to the canvas in just the right place for each color to make its own statement. Then we can stand back and visually integrate what on close inspection proves to be an intricate mixture of pigments. I even enjoy what the close inspection tells me of the method and skill of the artist, wondering as an aspiring painter if I will ever acquire that skill.

My lawn is a little bit like that to me. At a distance, except for certain brief periods of the year, it looks deceptively like every other lawn in the neighborhood. It takes a bit of concentration to spot its subtle diversity. But then on close-up inspection, the skill of the artist is revealed: the remarkable radial symmetry of the heads of dandelion and hawkweed, the interesting asymmetry of veronica and mint. Then there's the exquisite filigree of the leaves of yarrow, wild carrot, and mayweed. I can't think of a moment when I would choose to trade these for the linear uniformity of a blade of grass or the scurfy angularity of its fruiting panicles.

I believe the Lord concurs with this assessment. After all, it's his creation. All I do is cause the mower to be applied with regularity. Admittedly there's some selectivity, but it has little effect except to assure a regular recycling of herbs and a display of all that is beautiful and interesting there.

I'd like to point out in parting that I am actually a great admirer of grass. Grass contributes mightily to our welfare. For instance, corn, wheat, and rice are members of the grass family. Other forms of grass provide life and stability to many inhospitable environments, and a lawn without grass would be hard to maintain and would probably require more than mowing to keep it stable. For me, the optimum is three or four grass plants per square inch and at least one germinating chickweed seed or resprouting veronica plant.

I realize that mine is an eclectic view with few adherents, but I still feel moved to put in a word for the dandelion and its associates. Aldo Leopold has reminded us that education may sometimes be a matter of trading awareness for things of lesser worth. "The goose who trades his [awareness]," he says, "is soon a pile of feathers."

See, that's what my nature writing is really about: maintaining awareness and presenting diversified assessments of worth. The person who trades away his awareness of nature may soon become a goose.

The Romance of the Egg

Most people, when asked what makes a bird unique, would cite such things as birds can fly, or birds have feathers, maybe even birds sing.

Of course, the only definitive answer there is the one about feathers. Feathers are the unique characteristic of birds. Still, when I am asked that question about the uniqueness of birds, I tend to think of the egg and the care of young, neither of which are unique to birds. It's not what they do, but the way that they do it that catches my fancy.

There is great diversity across the spectrum of bird life. Consider incubation periods. They may vary from one and one half weeks for cowbird, house sparrow, and red-winged blackbird on one end of the scale, and eleven weeks for albatross and kiwi, that strange wingless bird of New Zealand, at the other end. Our birds can be divided into two basic categories: perching birds where the incubation period averages two weeks or slightly more, and non-perching birds, averaging from three to five weeks. Some baseline figures might be useful. Whistling swan and bald eagle take five weeks; Canada goose and turkey four weeks; woodpecker, robin, house wren, oriole, and cardinal are incubated about two weeks.

In general these categories also include two different types of hatchlings. Most birds with long incubation periods tend to hatch young able to run around and feed themselves within hours of hatching. *Precocial*, with obvious ties to *precocious*, is the term used.

First aired on WRVO-FM, June 23, 1989.

The short-incubation hatchlings are all relatively helpless and require anywhere from ten days to four weeks of care. *Altricial,* requiring feeding, is the term used here.

There are some interesting exceptions to this rule. Birds of prey, with four- to five-week incubation periods, have altricial hatchlings that may spend as many as ten weeks in the nest under the care of the adults. Herons, too, with a three- to four-week incubation period, still stay in or near the nest upwards of two weeks.

It is this variety of parental involvement that interests me most. Anyone watching a hen pheasant with a brood of chicks or a hen mallard with a half-dozen ducklings will tend to say, "Isn't she an attentive mother!" Indeed, she is, but duck and pheasant have it easy compared to the house wren or the robin, which will find its waking hours for anywhere from two to two and one half weeks filled with a constant search for food to placate seemingly insatiable offspring. Most songbird hatchlings require more than their weight in food each day.

Normally both sexes participate in food gathering. The intensity of this feeding varies somewhat with the time of day and the age of the young but may peak at 500 to 700 feeding trips per day with small songbirds.

Exceptional patterns of feeding and care would certainly include those of the moorhen and the black tern, both of which I studied in some detail years ago. The moorhen frequently lays a dozen eggs, which it begins to incubate soon after the third or fourth egg is laid. As a result, the first day of hatching may produce three or four precocial young with one egg hatching each subsequent day for a week or more. Since the young are able to move about and must eat soon after hatching, this presents quite a problem to the nest-bound female. At this point, however, the male takes charge of the hatchlings, squiring them about the nearby wetland as they forage for food and directing them with a single sharp note to seek cover and freeze.

When I first began to observe black terns nesting, I thought them somewhat neglectful as parents. The young seemed largely unattended as I observed them from screening cover. I soon learned, however, that the adult had things well in hand, constantly patrolling overhead and directing the activities of the chicks with vocal signals to freeze or forage. Recalcitrant young were buzzed, if not actually struck, to bring them in line. Meanwhile, every time I picked up a chick to band it or weigh it I received a sound thwack myself.

All of this comes to mind because of a brood of bluebirds being raised in a box at the edge of the lawn at Baltimore Woods. The female lost her mate before the brood was halfway along. This doubled her work as she made as many as six trips in fifteen minutes with food for the young.

Wild parents are almost always completely devoted to their roles as parents, but the nature of that devotion is only as deep as the traditions of their kind demand. The female bluebird had no choice. Without her, the nestlings would have perished.

The female bluebird lost her mate before the brood was halfway along.

Springtime Symphony

The interpreter must beware lest he read into his subject elements that are more the product of heart than mind. Heeding this warning, I still maintain there is music in the grand passage of spring, a symphony seemingly orchestrated by chance but still harmonious as any product of the cycles of nature must be.

It is a symphony with a classic theme, but its mode of presentation is more contemporary, in the style of jazz, a pastiche of ad-lib choruses in which each performer, intent on his own devices, seems oblivious of the others. Unplanned and uncoordinated as it may be, however, it is saved from chaos by some magic that only nature can comprehend. The blend is charming and uplifting, the effect enhanced by the fact that this is a premier performance. Since time immemorial, each spring morning has been greeted by a new performance, no two exactly alike.

It starts as we leave the house. A chorus of robins is greeting the sunrise. No matter that a layer of heavy stratus clouds obscures the sun and dampens the atmosphere, the robins are celebrating a moment precious to all life, the dawning of a new day. They do not need to see the sun to know that it is there. Their song is upbeat, even rollicking.

At this point, a mourning dove lays down his lugubrious legato. It provides a sobering minor undertone, starting and ending with a murmur and swelling to a full voice in the middle. Other doves join in, providing a growing musical disclaimer to the robin's joyous paean.

The combination provides a flute-clarinet duet. The robin's carol

Originally published in the *Baldwinsville Messenger,* May 2, 1979.

is upper register while the dove's alto notes are definitely lower register. Theirs is a spirited competition, building to a crescendo that is punctuated by the cymbal-like crow of a cock pheasant. Perhaps this is the doves' cue. They move to more distant coverts, their calls fading in the distance. The robins continue, completing the prelude. Their complementary passages provide a counterpoint that ebbs and flows like a bubbling brook.

I enter the evergreens on the way to the pond. The prelude gradually fades, replaced by a second movement built upon the framework of a reedy chorus of red-winged blackbirds and grackles. It is almost atonal and therefore less melodious than the prelude. As we draw nearer to the pond, the amphibian chorus joins in. The leopard frogs are sounding a basso continuo. It is a monotonous movement, sometimes punctuated by the piping of a spring peeper or the high-pitched trill of an American toad. There is something primal about this wetlands chorus. Its music speaks of the origins of life. This is its musical message, for it has no melody.

Across the pond, a song sparrow's solo beckons. It is the introduction to the next movement, an upland passage that we must seek out if we are to hear it. The wetlands chorus is eternal. It knows no respite this early in the morning, so we must provide its finale by moving out of earshot into the uplands.

We follow the song sparrow's lead and soon pick up the dulcet trill of the field sparrow. His is a sweet-voiced roll trailing off at the end, pausing a moment, and then recommencing. At the midpoint of the movement, the clarion call of a cardinal is interpolated like lacework around the fabric of the sparrow's song. Further along, a flicker inserts its winnowing eight-bar solo, and then a meadowlark claims the stage with a series of wild, high-pitched glissandos. From the top of a spruce tree at field's edge, a purple finch offers its sweet chatty warble. As we continue along, the whole chorus of field birds is joined, punctuated by the clanging cymbal voice of the cock pheasant.

It is time to return, and as I retrace my steps I am treated to a reprise of the wetlands chorus as the robin and mourning dove provide a fitting coda. At this point, I become aware of a bone-chilling dimension to this early morning concert. My feet are wet and my fin-

The prelude fades, replaced by a reedy chorus of red-winged blackbirds and grackles.

gers stiff, so I enter the house where, over a cup of coffee, I can reflect on my version of this springtime symphony.

I find I must deal with the question of whether this symphony is too contrived, its fabric constructed entirely on a man-made loom. Have I fabricated it from my head and the way I moved around?

Of course, any commentary on nature is man-made, but this did all happen, and not at my bidding. I am reporting to you on events observed and heard, and even had I spent all my time in one spot there would have been a diverting ebb and flow of natural sounds. To say that they are not music is to ignore the deep and lyric biotic pulses that have provided the unwritten score. If there is music anywhere in the natural world, surely it is here where the natural biologic events call for vocal expression.

Honk Once If You Agree

Across the Central New York countryside, spring is settling in and producing a remarkable transformation on the landscape. Just this morning on my way to one of my writing havens, I took the scenic routes, roads well-known to the denizens of northwest Onondaga County as Foster Road, Crossett Road, Fikes Road, and Whiting Road. These are roads with sections of distinct rural aspect where the plow and the cow still control more of the landscape than does the lawnmower. Where bluebirds and meadowlarks still nest and where backcountry white-tails have been joined by wild turkeys along the wooded ridges.

A certain variety is provided by expanses of broad creek bottom that flood in early spring and retreat to narrow pockets of wetland by summer. It is possible to accumulate a respectable bird count from the driver's seat of a slow-moving automobile without endangering the lives of tardy commuters who infest the primary roads, those who are not going to get to work on time if they obey speed limits and observe the niceties of highway etiquette.

I've learned that there is a subsection of the vocabulary that is reserved for gray-haired men who observe or underachieve the speed limits. It starts with something like "Why don't you get off the road, you old blankety-blank." These euphemisms are designed to suggest certain states of being that no dictionary has seen fit to accept or propagate, as yet.

I once had an opportunity to engage in friendly dialogue with

First aired on WRVO-FM, May 22, 1994.

one of my haranguers as we waited in a slow-moving line at a local convenience store. He didn't recognize me until I asked why he had been so angry at me just a few miles back. After a brief episode of embarrassment, he protested, saying that he wasn't angry but he did think that old people who had no serious reason for being there should keep away from the main traffic arteries. He wasn't sure that old people like me (he didn't make it that personal) should even have a license. At least he thought we ought to have yearly driver's tests. I pointed out politely that my age class had a better driving safety record than his, and that I personally had been driving since 1940 and had a record of over three-quarters of a million miles with only one minor traffic accident. He obviously didn't believe this, but since he was a very polite and respectful young man, he quickly retreated from a discussion where he wasn't making any points and I wasn't making any impression.

There are some things you need to understand about roadside bird watchers. Our slow pace doesn't mean we are ignoring traffic, even though in a very real sense we are trying to avoid it. Second, it isn't true that our good safety records are due to the fact that slow drivers who cause accidents usually escape being involved in them. I accept on faith the premise that bird watchers and other slow drivers are uncommonly lucky. Otherwise we'd be disappearing at the same precipitous rate as the birds we're trying to watch.

Now, I know you are getting frustrated trying to relate this introductory paean to spring in northwest Onondaga County with my annual defense of slow driving. Here's my point: An important condition of good citizenship, in my mind, is a proper appreciation of the marvelous variety and productivity of the landscape that nourishes us, both materially and spiritually. If you are one of those who believe, like sheep, that speed limits were created for lesser folks and that those who observe them are traffic hazards, your good citizenship, nay your common sense is suspect. The seat of an automobile should not be a combat-mentality zone.

This said, I would still, for the sake of polite young men who lose their cool when their pace of progress is slowed, recommend that we old timers adopt a code of roadside ethics. Before I propose the code, I'd like to point out that anyone who has graying hair or is approaching middle age is in danger of being classed as an old you-know-what by men and women just entering their twenties. Be aware that you may be a red flag to them.

My code: Don't drive too slow along the main access roads between home and work, especially during rush hours. If you pull over to let tailgaters go by, don't immediately pull back onto the highway right behind them. This may seem like a tacet criticism of their driving. People don't like that.

So I say search out roads like Fikes, and Foster and Whiting and others that curve and bump. Do it real soon. It's that time of the year. If you see a car with a bumper sticker that says "Start early and enjoy the land that feeds you," that's me. Honk once if you agree with me and twice if you find my erratic pace annoying. I'll get the message.

The Calico Fields

It is in late May when the viburnums, the dogwoods (silky, red osier, graystem, and alternate leaved), and the black locust have drawn attention to the hedgerows. This is an annual event, not to be ignored by the true lover of the sights, sounds, and aromas of spring. Still, I'd hate to see you so preoccupied with the hedgerows that you ignore the emergence of the calico fields.

I am referring here to the recently abandoned or indifferently tended meadow or fallowed field. It is here that rocket, dandelion, fleabane, and campion have produced a spotted tapestry of green, pale gold, pink, and white, as striking as the mottled cotton prints that the term *calico* usually calls to mind.

There are two ways to view the calico fields. From afar, as from a slow-moving or even from a parked automobile, or from up close, as from fawn's eye or even from worm's eye view. Either viewpoint takes a bit of orientation, but both are necessary if the message of the calico fields is to be fully appreciated. This is a case where a rural background is not really an advantage because, let's face it, folks, we're talking here about weeds again. It takes a bit of sophistication and a bit of detachment for the farmer to see beauty in a field liberally spotted with weeds.

With that much introduction, let's look first at the calico field from a distance. Since most aspects of agriculture are based on monoculture, the nurture of one species of plant per field, no cockle in the corn field, no mustard in the oat field, the well-tended field has

First aired on WRVO-FM, May 29, 1987.

a uniformity of color and texture about it. Withhold the mower or the plow or the cattle for just a year, however, and the calico pattern begins to appear. It may be the pink and white of musk mallow slavishly aligned with the old tillage patterns to start with. Ere long, indiscriminately placed patches of pale yellow rocket, buttercup, or hawkweed will infuse the fields, intermixed soon with the white or pale pink of campion and the blue of speedwell, violet, and varied mints.

The ultimate in caliconess, if there is such a thing, is introduced by dame's rocket, a plant that will grow in the sunbathed open fields or in the shaded fringes of the hedgerows. The colors of this showy member of the mustard clan provide a complex of pastel shades that is distinctly modern. Like so many of these invaders of the neglected field, the rocket, which some people call wild phlox, is an alien. It cannot, I believe, trace its American ancestry even halfway back to the Plymouth landing of the Mayflower.

This is only a small sampling of the many field flowers that invade the springtime meadows. Since most of the early invaders are pale in color or diminutive in stature, they are not as evident or as memorable as the sequences of blooms that follow. Orange daylily, sky blue chicory, pinkish purple loosestrife, lacy white Queen Anne's lace, and gold and white daisy punctuate the deepening mantle of the summer field.

It must be a time of great confusion for the honey bee, which likes to concentrate on one source of nectar until that supply is exhausted. Fortunately, however, the summer insect population is legion. There never seems to be a shortage of pollinators.

That the honeybee concentrates on the speciation of the calico field is a reminder of the second way to view the field, the bee's eye view. If we examine the field as the bee does, from flower to flower, we discover a second kind of treasure, that of form and function. It is a fact that the flowers of the field are as exquisite in form as any that can be found in the best-tended garden. Take along a magnifying glass. No bloom in the calico field becomes less interesting or less attractive under magnification.

The graceful little field chickweed, its dainty petals cleft almost to their base, shows five dull brown and five bright salmon anthers, a lovely little surprise. The stamens of the golden wood sorrel unite at their bases to form a tube surrounding the pistil. You have to search among the taller weeds to locate them. There, among the bases of the taller weeds, you may locate the purple four-lipped trumpets of gill-over-the-ground. You'd never see them from your automobile.

Next direct your lens to the golden heads of Canada hawkweed. You may not even have to bend down to view the flowers. What you discover is that the hawkweed bloom is really a complex of strap-shaped flowers, each linear flowerlet accompanied by a tall slender pistil with gracefully curved stigmas at the summit.

Believe me, if you have any eye for form at all, you'll not regret a few moments spent examining the floral denizens of the calico field at close range.

Observing Summer

The wind
is whispering
Softly in the marshgrass
Safely in my arms
My baby sleeps
    Sleeps.

Sir Bullfrog
chugarumphing
in deep harmony
To Page Peeper
Safely in my arms
My baby sleeps
    Sleeps.

The moon
rising high
Sprays pale silver shining
On all the meadow folk below
While safely in my arms
My baby sleeps
    Sleeps. —JWD

The hallmark of summer in Central New York is greenness and growth. If we could measure its total energy conversion, we would find it even more explosive than spring. However, its general energy level is so high that we scarcely notice the changes occurring.

The engine of summer is operating in high gear. Its velocity increases until the gradual southward migration of the sun begins to restrict its fuel supply. Summer peaks sometime in late July or early August when the adult waterfowl are in their eclipse plumage, the swallows are congregating prior to migration, and the bell curve of reproduction is nearly completed.

Summer brings heat, spectacular cloud formations, and the ripening of spring's botanical initiatives. Included are many rites of passage, but none is more interesting than the transfer of the spectacular flower shows from the woodlands to the fields and wetlands.

The summer weed fields, ditches, and field edges assume a patchwork pattern of yellows, pinks, reds, and blues. The same colors will appear in the shallows of marshes and river bottoms. The whole is reminiscent of calico cloth, so I have named them the calico fields. Although the fields begin to bloom in late spring, no one seems to notice. The woodlands are still too colorful. As summer matures, the taller perennials such as goldenrod and aster begin to dominate, producing meadows deep with gold and purple and white.

There are several ways to observe summer. One can find in the home lives of birds, mammals, and insects the lessons of the survival of species. One can consider the nearly infinite variety of plant form and function. Perhaps most revealing of all is to observe the intricate interplay between plant and animal life. Study those interactions for lessons about the strategies of community well-being.

Summer ends when growth ceases and harvest is due. Most people in Central New York would agree that summer is not really over until October.

Touring Nature's Garden by Canoe

This is the season of maturing dreams, when the seeds we so carefully placed in well-worked ground two months earlier have finally proven their fruitful potential.

Our gardens, even those indifferently tended, are producing in abundance. Our backs, previously aching from the tasks of cultivation, now accept a more welcome burden, the harvest. The garden has a special place in the saga of man that is somewhat upstaged by the bulging produce bins of modern supermarkets. Still, the fruitful garden and the bulging produce bins are civilized mirrors of the general condition of nature in August.

The marsh, which many suspect is my favorite garden, has its own abundance of an August morning. It is an entirely different scene from springtime when migrant birds mingled with already nesting birds produce a carnival of sound and movement. The snores, trills, and peeps that filled the spring night have been replaced by the plunk of green frog and chugarum of bull frog. Vegetation stands low over the springtime marsh. The displays of blooms are not of the dominant plants and will be overtopped ere long.

Let's visit an August marsh to see what is ready for visual harvest. We'll take along a canoe, for even though water levels drop in summer, there will still be places where it is knee-deep or more. We approach the marsh through a soggy field alive with pink blooms of swamp milkweed, a happy blending of delicate color and exquisite form.

Originally published in the *Baldwinsville Messenger*, Aug. 11, 1976.

In a shallow draw, joe-pye weed spreads its frothy pinkish blooms head high above the fringing sedge meadow. The sedges are productive but unspectacular. Their heavy nodding spikes are dull brown or straw colored, but here and there are dense clumps of golden burr marigold still blooming and providing a reminder that plant life is in reality bottled sunlight. We avoid these plants because their barbed two-pronged sticktights are ready for business.

We launch the boat in an open bay scattered with mats of elegant white water lilies. We pause to admire a single bloom; its radiating velvet petals stand above a cartwheel of tapering green sepals. At the center is a golden cluster of stamens. Presently honey bees are poring over these pollen-laden spires. They leave heavily burdened with their golden harvest but haven't made a dent on the abundant supply. The shiny dark green lily leaves look like deeply cleft platters. A gentle breeze occasionally upends a leaf, showing its purplish undersurface. We pole along between seven-foot walls of cattails, their cylindrical brown fruiting heads like impaled cigars nodding in the gentle breeze.

Suddenly the air is split with the squawk of a gallinule. We look

We launched the boat in an open bay scattered with mats of elegant white water lilies.

just in time to see this large gray rail and its half grown family disappear behind the cattail curtain. It is a strange bird, apparently half duck and half chicken but actually neither. In August it is the voice of the marsh. The gallinules have been gleaning a clump of arrowhead in search of snails. Again we stop to examine the narrow triangular leaves and waxy white blooms. They are not as spectacular as the lily, each bloom being less than an inch in diameter, but have a delicate grace and beauty.

The gallinules have barely faded from view when we become aware of the soft gabbles, chuckles, and quacks of feeding ducks. We push our way through a narrow channel and enter into a secluded bay. There a dozen drake mallards in various stages of molt are loafing on floating logs or feeding on the seeds of pondweed. They hurriedly retreat into the vegetation but leave behind the evidence of what they are about. The water is covered with feathers.

It is also covered with rosettes of narrow floating leaves. From the center of each rosette grows a single dark stalk with an oval cluster of magenta blooms, the water smartweed. Honey bees are working these blooms, too. We watch for a moment, and then our attention is drawn to the water. It is alive with an incredible mixture of creatures from microscopic animalcules to a foot-long pickerel. He pauses at the surface long enough to be seen and then darts away. The more we look, the more we see, but there isn't time to dwell on anything. There's too much more to see.

We are approaching the far side of the marsh when a strange bird, the size of a large chicken, flushes awkwardly from the water. Its long neck and long legs identify it as the American bittern, a member of the heron family. It had been standing in plain sight but was camouflaged by its tawny striped plumage and its habit of standing ramrod straight and reed tall with bill pointed heavenward.

The lagoon in which the bittern had been searching for minnows is fringed by a particularly attractive bed of purple pickerelweed and the tall nodding white spires of lizard's tail. The rich green foliage topped with spires of purple and white makes as fine a bed of blooms as I have seen in any upland garden. We move on, traversing a passageway between the cattails, and emerge in a swampy lagoon overtopped by black willows. A half grown brood of wood ducks skitters across the water and disappears among the clumps of huge-leaved arums.

We shift our focus to a spit on the shoreline where we behold a breathtaking sight, a clump of blood-red cardinal flower basking in a patch of noonday sun. Tall, graceful, and unbelievably rich, it is a feature of the marshland garden without peer. Then, as if to prove that anything can be topped, we note a hummingbird busily probing the brilliant blooms. He twists and turns like a bright green jewel. Suddenly, just before he darts away, we are treated for a brief moment to the ruby glow of his throat patch, perhaps the only thing in nature that can rival the cardinal flower for redness. A feathered gem, indeed!

It is time to turn back now, and we've really just begun to describe the wonders of the marshland garden. We have said nothing about the edible harvest that made the marsh of prime value to Native American or knowledgeable pioneer. Today we rate the marsh much lower on our value scale. Despite wetland legislation to protect the marshes, many are still attempting to eliminate and occupy them, frequently to their sorrow when unplanned flooding of their dwellings results.

Those few of us who view the marsh with the eyes of the pioneer would like to enter into the record books this account of the abundant harvest that the August marsh provides.

The Hummingbird!

Minute, Mighty, Magical

If I were to ask you what bird weighs in at one-one hundred sixtieth of a pound, is no longer than your index finger, can magically change from dull gray to sparkling ruby red and iridescent green in an instant, and can perform aerial maneuvers that would put the honeybee to shame, you probably wouldn't pause long over the answer. Hummingbirds, truly a New World product, can outshine and outmaneuver any other group of birds you've ever seen, hands down.

For all of their secretiveness and diminutive stature, hummingbirds are well-known and well-loved. People plan their patios or courtyard gardens to attract them and go to great lengths to draw them within arm's length. In return, the hummingbird displays a winning combination of demureness and fearlessness.

Fascination with these birds predates the time when Sir Walter Raleigh's Captain Barlowe described the ruby-throat as an "amayzing insecte." Even in Colonial times, people weren't quite sure about the proper classification of this tiny bird, especially when they saw it apparently consorting with sphinx moths as large as or larger than they and quite similar in general appearance.

Anyone who watches them very long will soon see that the darting, aggressive hummer operates on an entirely different plane from any insect. That is due in part to its warm-bloodedness and in part to its more sophisticated brain.

First aired on WRVO-FM, July 14, 1994.

We have about fifteen species of hummingbirds in the continental forty-eight states, but only the ruby-throated variety tends to spend much time east of the Mississippi. The bird's breeding range extends from Nova Scotia and Montana south to the Mexican border. The annual migration of the eastern ruby-throats calls for a 500-mile crossing of the Gulf of Mexico to its wintering areas in Central America.

Everyone with whom I have shared this information finds it just barely believable. Many people find it easier to believe that the bird hibernates in some protected nook. That is far from the truth, but the kind of deep sleep that characterizes hibernation is not unknown to hummingbirds. Their tiny size dictates such a high rate of metabolism that deep sleep, with lowered rates of body function and temperature, is required to tide them over from bedtime to breakfast.

Every hummingbird must consume over half its weight in energy-rich foods during its waking hours. When she has hungry nestlings to feed, the female is a feathered dynamo. Her energetic foraging for food borders on the frantic. She appears and disappears time and again, systematically working over the larkspur, bee balm, coral bells, and other brightly colored tubular annuals and perennials.

The hummingbird's energetic foraging for food borders on the frantic.

The performance seems almost ritualistic, but those who believe hummingbirds never rest have not watched them carefully enough. Every foray includes a brief period of rest, usually on the same perch. That has been my experience, at least.

As for size, the hummingbird is one-half inch shorter than the tiny goldfinch. About a quarter of its length consists of a slim tubular bill, which it uses like a straw to extract nectar and tiny insects from flowers. In the shade, the bird may seem drab, but when it catches the reflected light of the sun, it glows and glints with bright green. The ultimate surprise, however, is the throat of the male, which can seem to change color from charcoal to blood red in a twinkling. The effect is electric.

My fondness for the hummer is based mostly on its colorful behavior. I have watched the male swing back and forth in a huge arc, fly up, fly down, and even backward. I have observed aggressive face-to-face ritual flights and have even seen a hummer attack a Cooper's hawk that apparently ventured into its written-on-the-wind territory.

Truly the bird is a nonpareil with whom you might wish to cultivate an acquaintance.

The Sad Plight of the Bobolink

The bobolink is a bird that has prospered and declined at the hands of man. In primeval times, its numbers were concentrated in those parts of North America where prairie grasses predominated. To find comparable wintering grounds, it traveled all the way south to the pampas of Brazil and Argentina, an excessively long trip by many standards, but nowhere near as hazardous a journey then as it is today.

In the eastern United States, any bobolinks that may have existed would have been at the mercy of such elements as wildfire, disease, high wind, high water, and the buffalo: anything that could remove the forest and keep it from reasserting itself. Bobolinks were scarce, it seems, over much of the northeast.

Then came the European invasion and the introduction of plowing and tilling methods that opened new vistas for bobolinks. This was a different kind of agriculture than that practiced by the Native Americans, and although the Europeans learned much about the land from the natives they rapidly displaced, they set about to change the face of eastern North America. Their methods, designed to accommodate livestock, put a premium on pasture and meadow, the latter of which was home ground for the bobolink.

By the middle of the nineteenth century, the bobolink had accomplished an amazing eastward shift in population. How much of this was due to the precipitous decline of the bison, I can't say. The bobolink apparently experienced a population decline in the north-

First aired on WRVO-FM, Aug. 5, 1994.

east after 1850, but *Birds of New York,* published in 1908, lists the bobolink as common-to-abundant in all upstate counties dominated by agriculture. Even though its population fluctuated in the northeast, at least in central New York the bobolink had tied its star to the mower and the reaper. It nested in the hayfields and dined on ripe grains and weed seeds to prepare it for that long trip to the Argentine.

Over the decades, the bobolink became increasingly addicted to hayfields where grasses abound in preference to mature clearings where the dominance of grasses and certain weeds was very fleeting and there was no cutting to remove litter. This would have been fine indefinitely had it not been for the changes in meadow management that followed World War II.

When I was young, it was deemed important for the hay to cure before it was stored. Green hay, unbaled and crammed into the hay mow, was like a time bomb. Temperature sufficient to ignite the cured hay could build up within the pockets of less well-cured hay leading to spontaneous combustion and fires, which sometimes would wipe out a building complex including farm machinery and livestock. In those days, haying was delayed until late June; however, today baling and the ensiling of green-chop hay has resulted in early and frequent harvest of the meadow.

Here's an example that I watched this year. Close to Baltimore Woods on a side road off New Seneca Turnpike is a fifteen-acre hayfield. Early in May, it became clear that two pairs of bobolinks had settled in to nest. I made frequent trips there to confirm this good news. Always, one or both of the males were to be seen coursing over the meadow, wings beating rapidly, delivering their energized flight songs, one supposes to mates concealed in the grasses and meadow weeds and to rival males to demonstrate their territorial boundaries. Imagine my delight in being able to watch this handsome bird.

It is somewhat smaller than the red-winged blackbird, with black underparts, a white-striped back, and a buff-colored hind neck. Whether in flight or on a favorite perch, the bird delivers its rapid-fire song with a spate of energy matched only by the house wren. The female is sparrowlike in appearance. Its nest is placed deep among the grasses, a grassy cup that usually harbors four or five eggs, light bluish profusely spotted and blotched with brown.

Because of its well-concealed location and the habit of the birds of alighting at a distance from the nest and taking a concealed pathway to it, the nest is difficult to find. But despite the constant attendance of the birds in this meadow, it seems doubtful that those two pairs fledged any young. The first cutting of the hay came too soon for the young to have reached fledgling state. The second cutting, now accomplished, appears to have been too soon to allow for successful re-nesting.

This dilemma of timing, plus changes in its wintering ground and massive meadow abandonment hereabouts, gives great concern about the future for bobolinks. What was once our commonest true meadow bird is increasingly hard to find. Let's hope it can adjust to the changes.

Nature's Predators Serve a Purpose

One thing we transfer from our own lives to nature is the tendency to select heroes and villains. In nature, the kingbird and the hummingbird are the heroes because both fearlessly attack the hunting Cooper's hawk, who is without a second thought cast in the role of the villain. Other widely considered villains include the crow, weasel, coyote, and that villain of all villains, the sly fox. Our folk customs have invested the fox with the ultimate aura of villainy, slyness, duplicity, and cold calculating bloodthirstiness.

All of this is understandable, but it is also naive. In nature, the predator has his own mandate and role. The mandate is to survive, using the equipment that is provided. The role is to provide a balance against the excessive reproductive capacity of its prey species.

Think of it. Unchecked, species like the field mouse or rabbit would increase to the point of destruction of its food supply. In the consequent starvation, these almost totally vegetarian creatures would not be the only sufferers. This kind of self-destructive outbreak is the classic example of plague, except that plague is a device of humankind. In nature, plague is really more a matter of population adjustment, in which a dysfunctional wild community takes a logical route to becoming functional again. The principal ways of achieving adjustment are epidemic disease, starvation, or emigration.

In nature, however, there is one other means of achieving adjustment. As populations of prey species grow, predators concentrate on those areas of excessive population increase. If they are successful in

First aired on WRVO-FM, June 30, 1994.

The bobcat's role is to balance the numbers of its prey species.

removing the peaks in the growth curve, the impending disaster may be averted.

In primeval America, where the Native American was both spiritually and physically a part of the environment, this system normally worked. When the European immigrant arrived 300 years ago, bringing a whole different folklore and system of value judgments, the predators soon found themselves to be villains, no longer able to follow their professions unhindered. Predator control became the rule in every frontier community. The first motive was to protect domestic animals. The results were often unfortunate, however, and should have been instructive.

We have many classic examples of the folly of predator extirpation, but none more impressive than in deer populations around the country. Except during brief rutting seasons, most deer species have a high tolerance for others of their kind. Therefore, as populations grow, there is no warning signal to pressure the thinning of numbers by emigration. They all just stay in one place until food supplies are nearly destroyed and starvation follows.

The results can be devastating. I can think of nothing in nature that has been more distressful for me to observe than the results of mass starvation. People who believe that population control by predation is a cruel device have their priorities somewhat misplaced. In the grand scheme of things, we can see that natural factors that tend to prevent such disasters should hardly be classed as villainous, and their principal agents—the hawk, the owl, the weasel, and the fox—should not be cast out of the community.

In nature, reproductive capacity is always designed to outstrip functional population levels. This surplus is the logical food supply for predators. To deny them this is to frustrate a grand design intended to ensure the health of wild populations.

When we consider the predator's equipment, talons, hooked bills, aggressiveness, swiftness of foot or wing, and sharp teeth unsuited for chewing of vegetation, we can see that the creator, or the grand design if you prefer, honors the role of the predator.

Butterflies That Flutter By

The calico fields are at their best right now with patches of mullein, hawksbeard, mallow, susan, and bellflower to give them life. These bright blooms call forth a second array of blossoms, these with the power of flight. They go by such names as monarch, admiral, viceroy, and fritillary. These meetings of sedentary field flowers and peripatetic butterflies are symbiotic, the epitome of mutual benefit: one gets food lapped up through its retractable straw, the other gets pollen with which to fertilize its expectant seed.

Strange name, butterfly. I have no idea of its origin. Some nature lovers hold that it is a corruption of flutterby, which they hold to be a superior name for these energetic insects. Sounds a bit too pat, doesn't it. At any rate, butterflies are part of a large group of insects said to contain over 120 thousand species worldwide, and known collectively as the Lepidoptera, the moths and butterflies. Lepidoptera is a term of Greek origin that, literally translated, means "scaled wing." It is the tiny flat scales covering their wings like shingles that give them their bright color.

I've been mildly interested in butterflies and moths as long as I can remember. The result is that while I celebrate their presence each year as the calico fields brighten, I'm not a true student who immediately pulls out the field guide. This is good. Butterflies give me enormous pleasure with a minimum of vexation. There are said to be about 700 species of butterflies in North America, many of them tropical. That provides the substance for an interesting variety of color, form, and function.

First aired on WRVO-FM, July 20, 1990.

Butterflies That Flutter By | 91

A great many people share my casual interest in butterflies. That was evident on a recent trip to Georgia when we visited the butterfly house at Calloway Gardens. What an experience! Imagine a glass-covered dome, over three stories high, crammed with lush vegetation, brilliantly adorned with a spectrum of blooms. Then imagine clouds of butterflies, no less brilliantly colored, freely circulating throughout this huge vivarium. Very impressive!

Now imagine crowds of people plying the trails that wind through the vegetation, stopping to admire a scarlet and black butterfly perched momentarily on leaf or blossom. Cameras click. There is a constant undertone of *ooh*s and *ah*s. At least a half dozen people at any one time are fortunate enough to have a butterfly perch briefly on head, or arm or shoulder. Many recoil at first, but all are soon proudly displaying their visitors to a crowd of interested bystanders.

I can imagine that some lepidopterists might look askance at such a show-biz atmosphere, but to this educator, who believes that the first step in the learning process is building awareness, it was an impressive show. Butterflies were in the minds of these people, so they watched film clips and studied interpretive exhibits.

What the displays pointed out bears repeating. The life cycle of a butterfly, or a moth for that matter, is a complex pathway. The butterfly starts out life encased in a tiny, often exquisitely sculpted or tinted egg deposited by the female on the ground or on carefully selected host plants. Butterflies are most often very host-specific. What emerges from the egg is a wormlike caterpillar, a true eating machine, which systematically attacks wild carrot, milkweed, willow, or cherry—each to the preference of its clan.

Caterpillars grow rapidly and are soon ready to transform into a fancifully shaped pupal case known as a chrysalis. This sarcophagus-like structure is a rigid box, seemingly a place of enforced quiet. Actually it is a time of profound interior activity as worms turn into butterflies. The considerable energy consumed is the product of the caterpillar's diligent feeding.

When the butterfly emerges, it is a transformed creature both in form and function. Its mouth parts are no longer designed for chewing. It is now fitted with a retractable straw; its food nectar rather than leaf tissue. The important events in its life, now, will be mating and egg laying, the assurance of a new generation to enliven future calico fields.

It's a good time to take a trip to the calico fields in search of flutterbys. Swallowtails, all of varying amounts of black, yellow, and blue or green with distinctive narrow tails projecting from the rear wings; or monarch, chestnut or burnt sienna with spotted black fringes on the wings; or fritillaries, their rusty colored wings spotted and blotched with umber and white; or perhaps brightly marked admirals, their dark wings prominently marked with broad white bars. Or perhaps their near relative, the viceroy, a compact smaller edition of the monarch.

If you give them space and watch carefully, and I would recommend using binoculars, you'll discover unexpected rewards. The butterflies are an interesting lot.

The Story of a Tree

This is the story of a tree. It is just a common tree. *Acer saccharum*, sugar maple, state tree of New York State, almost as common as grass hereabouts. This tree's distinction, then, is not in its pedigree. Its lineage is good but not outstanding. Still, this tree meant a lot to my wife and me. Part of that special meaning rested in its location, just forty-five feet east-southeast of the house at the edge of Dublin Road. Along with its companions, two younger, less impressive specimens, it protected our house from the bright morning sun, helping to keep it ten degrees cooler inside on the dog days of July and August.

On a warm June morning from our bedroom window, we could hear the quiet conversation of leaves stirring in the gentle breeze. Robin, flicker, and blue jay greeted the sun from favored lofty perches. Within the tree's lofty crown were hidden assorted nests including robin, oriole, warbling vireo, and, one year, a red-eyed vireo that found in the tree's dense foliage a semblance of its normal forest haunts.

That's the other part of this tree's significance to me. It was no ordinary maple. In fact, it had within it the capacity to reach tape measure proportions. During the last decade of its life, this patriarch tree equaled the best growth of its vigorous youth. At eighty-six, this tree stood nearly eighty feet tall, its crown spanning over sixty feet and its circumference at breast height nearly twelve feet. This was a prominent tree with great potential for future growth, but it also had

First aired on WRVO-FM, Aug. 28, 1992.

Robin, flicker, and blue jay greeted the sun from favored lofty perches.

a flaw. Earlier in its life this tree had suffered damage; its bark cocoon had been breached and it hadn't ever completely recovered, a seemingly trivial flaw but one that might cause it to succumb to high wind or heavy snow sometime in the future.

Esther and I have known this tree for less than fifteen years, so it was with a feeling of great sorrow we learned that despite some early indications to the contrary, that magnificent specimen was to be sacrificed on the altar of progress. The highwaymen were at it again. The highwaymen, in fact, wear different costumes, in this case the blazers and logos of a local utility.

The tree, we learned, through no fault of its own, was in the way. It had to go and with it all the benefits it had bestowed on the people and on the wildlife who had occupied the space at Dublin Road, and even those who had driven by over the years.

We didn't struggle against the inevitable. Roads don't alter their courses even a fraction of an inch for common folk like us, and having been a bureaucrat myself for a substantial part of my career, I am well aware of the annoying difficulties unreasonable people can cause. No sense in being unreasonable in a losing cause. I'd prefer to save my adrenalin for things of greater import. Besides, I have the capacity to do for that tree something no highwayman can ever take away. I can give it a kind of immortality. As a result of one five-minute profile, I can provide it with instant renown, and perhaps someone reviewing these notes at some future date will gain a new insight into our times. This may be a hedge against Aldo Leopold's reminder that the world soon forgets the extinct organism, along with all the lessons it could teach.

If I had my way, no patriarch maple, which in its own silent way has witnessed so much history, would have to die without revealing its experiences. We can't afford to leave such worldly wisdom to the hills alone. What better message for a generation that is rapidly losing a sense of its dependance on the soil, the water, and the atmosphere and on the superb productions of the interactions of these three? That tree, no extremist, has a message born in its own exquisite intimacy with soil and air and the seasons. Some time I'll try to give a thumbnail sketch of what the tree told me as I crouched over its remnant stump measuring and remembering.

The Continuing Story of a Tree

My grand old maple tree became a foot-high stump and some seven and one half cords of firewood on August 11, 1992. When everything but the stump was removed the next day, leaving a gap in the shade like a missing tooth, I took my measuring equipment to try to learn something of its life.

As I looked at the stump, the first thing I noticed was that the trunk was not round but was fluted or scalloped. Four measurements taken from the core of the tree to the wide parts of these lobes showed an average radius of twenty-three inches. Four measurements taken from the core to the sinuses or indentations showed an average radius of almost eighteen inches. Using this calculation, the average diameter would be forty-one inches. Interestingly enough, if you use a forester's diameter tape, the average diameter would be forty-six inches because the tape misses the indentations.

After much counting and recounting, I have decided that the tree's date of birth, so to speak, was 1906. This would amount to an average diameter growth of about one-fifth of an inch per year in the sinuses and over one half inch diameter growth per year in the lobes. That's pretty good growth. What's more, during its last ten years of life, its growth topped the average for its younger years. Despite some weaknesses, this old patriarch was healthy.

Consider what the tree can tell us about its life and times. For the first six or seven years of its life, the tree was obviously in a seed bed or in some other crowded and shaded situation. Its diameter growth

First aired on WRVO-FM, Sept. 4, 1992.

of less than three-tenths of an inch per year shows that. Perhaps it was clipped back by rabbits or deer for several years before it escaped their attention. In fact, it didn't really start to show normal growth until its tenth year. That might suggest that it was planted on Dublin Road in about 1916, during World War I. At that time Dublin was still a dirt road, and the traffic it witnessed would have been a mixture of horse-drawn vehicles and various square-cut autos with European names such as Metz, Chevrolet, and LaVoiturette. Then, of course, there was the ultimate American car of its day, the Ford.

My maple was just three inches in diameter at that time and perhaps twenty feet in height. It overlooked the Dublin Road section of Howlett Hill Road, still gravel surface in 1915 but due to be paved the next year. It's not clear whether the tree's placement there preceded or followed the paving. It's a good bet, however, that the vehicles traveled by at speeds in excess of the fifteen mile per hour speed limit recently installed in the village (up from eight miles per hour).

Where my tree spent its first ten years is a matter of conjecture. Perhaps in the valley along the route of the Marcellus and Otisco Valley Railroad. Perhaps on the heights overlooking Otisco Lake where it could have monitored the daily cruises of the passenger boat Fontney, an aquatic extension of the railroad. My maple grew almost eight inches in diameter during the short life of the railroad. By 1930, it had achieved a diameter of nearly one foot and a height of perhaps forty feet. Our house was built about a decade earlier and the tree was planted to screen it from the road.

Sometimes I think we overlook the things a tree can do for us. For most of us it is shade and beauty, but to me a tree is an amazing botanical entity, a marvelous example of biological engineering. We take trees too much for granted. Why, my tree was as big as a whale, and unlike the whale, which lives in the supporting and cushioning water medium, that maple tree had to stand on end holding aloft tons of branches and foliage. Every year it did monumental work resisting winds and carrying snow loads in winter.

It is the strategy of the tree's design to allow this. The living, vulnerable part of the tree, the growth points, are always at the surface and peripheral. Only a thin overlayer of the trunk is functional in providing growth, passing raw materials aloft to the leaf-energy-foodstuff factory, and carrying the manufactured products to the storage areas. The rest of that massive, nearly four foot thick trunk served the function of strengthening and storage, providing a bole that could hold the factory aloft. In fact, the whole woody portion of the tree above and below the ground is ensheathed with a thin cloak of life, inside of which is the heartwood that provides its support.

Beneath the ground is a mass of roots, rootlets, and root hairs as extensive as the aerial part of the tree. The millions of root hairs are like myriad tiny mouths receiving moisture and nutrients. The rest of the root system, the internal woody part, anchors the tree to the ground. All of this so that the foliage factory can do its job consuming carbon dioxide, producing oxygen and tremendous amounts of carbohydrates, while housing birds and squirrels and bats and incidentally providing welcome shade for house and lawn.

Every tree that lives for eight decades is an encyclopedia of events and accomplishments. In a sense, cutting a tree is like burning a book. Unlike nature, which reuses all the material, we just throw much of it away. It's too bad these things don't mean more to us.

My August Walk in Baltimore Woods

The trails of Baltimore Woods provide a great showcase for all that is beautiful and interesting in the natural areas of Central New York. In spring, bloodroot, hepatica, and trillium grace the trailside. Now it's August and it's a different story.

For all their verdancy, the August woods are somehow drab by comparison with the May woods. The August woods are replete with the fulfillment of spring's promises. The blood-red fruits of baneberry and false Solomon's Seal, the globular fruiting bodies of the wild leek: these are part of that promise. A major function of baneberry, false Solomon's Seal, and leek would seem to be the production of seed-bearing fruits. An organism that doesn't prepare for future generations has scant promise of a future.

As I sit now about an hour before sunset on a sunny prominence overlooking but not actually in the woods, I can see where the bright colors of August reside. With few exceptions, they are in the fields, not in the woods. Still, I see a few things worthy of mention that weren't in evidence a few weeks ago, and a few that were there but didn't seem worth mentioning then.

First there is a spattering of miniature bachelor buttons, the knapweeds. Beautiful swatches of magenta. And at this hour, nothing is more prominent than the golden heads of black-eyed Susan, coneflower, and wild sunflower. Add to that the first vanguard of oceans of goldenrod. Along the way, I saw several spires of the angular sky blue blooms of great lobelia. We can look forward to several weeks of its lovely presence.

First aired on WRVO-FM, Aug. 8, 1986.

100 | Observing Summer

As I walked through the woods, I was impressed by the silence. A month ago, the streamside would have echoed with the vespers of the veery. Diligent searching might still have turned up its nest, probably without a clutch of china blue eggs. The veery is predominantly a ground nester, and its nests are really among the most comely in setting, nestled among the ferns and the Canada May flowers.

But now even the red-eyed vireo is silent. This doesn't mean there are no birds. I can hear the chortles of an agitated wood thrush. As the sun drops lower, he'll regale us with a few pure snatches of his bedtime lullaby. As I criss and cross the stream, a ruffed grouse explodes from right beneath my feet. I have a good view of him as he picks his way through the understory. A month ago he was still drumming just before sundown.

As I sit here now, a persistent chipping greets me. It's a familiar call. There's its author, the brightest bird of Baltimore Woods, a scarlet tanager. He's going to land in the top of that tall skinny maple about thirty feet away. What a sight! There's no real way to convey the richness of his velvety plumage. Just imagine the brightest of red accented by the deepest blue-black, and you'll have it. In the distance, perhaps from the corn fields over near Seneca Turnpike, a cock pheasant crows. Pleasant to hear its cymbal call after several years of absence.

I can hear the chortles of an agitated wood thrush.

I've been sitting here fully expecting the doe and twin fawns that inhabit this section of the woods to appear. I always expect to see deer when I walk these trails. That expectation is not always fulfilled, but the frequency of appearance is enough to keep the expectation alive.

The sun is approaching the horizon now. A flock of ducks flies across its path, and nearer a small group of waxwings completes its last pre-dusk flight. At that moment, the other special feature I always expect at Baltimore Woods, two handsome crow-sized pileated woodpeckers fly across the valley just above the tree tops. They land just out of sight, but their strident calls echo across the valley.

Then all is silent as the sun begins to sink beyond the hill. All, that is, except the flutelike song of the wood thrush.

There are still a few moments left before it becomes too dark to pick my way back through the woods. I can just sit quietly and watch as the sinking sun leaves the woods and concentrates on the high alto stratus and cirrus clouds as well as the contrail of a jet. It also catches another silver plane, this one with no sign at all of a trailing cloud. Just as I am about to leave, a multicolored balloon hovers into sight. Strange how those near silent evidences of civilization can break the wilderness mood.

Time to pack up my equipment and follow their lead back to the twentieth century.

Observing Autumn

Green valleys stretching wide
  with patchworking in brown
  and it's my home.
I've walked every inch of the
  valley.
Strayed from path and beaten trail
  (though I never passed
  them by without having
  tried them once).
Idled beside cold trickling
  streams
  and watched deer pass
  graceful,
  full of beauty.
My heart is here
  buried mid the dust
  will be eroded by the rains
  tempered by the winds and
  winter snows.
But never shall it be
  extracted nor extricated
For its roots are in the
  land

*deep in the earth
holding fast
and strong
to that which it holds
dear.* —JWD

Autumn is the reciprocal of spring. It is the sunset time of the year, as colorful and changeable as an autumn sundown and, measured against the total year, just as brief. All of this color bespeaks the harvest. First the leaves loose their hold on the branches and fall to the ground to cloak and enrich the soil. Their contribution will form the substance with which future springs are nourished.

Left behind are the apples and berries and fruiting heads of grain. They, too, will serve a dual role. They will provide the energy for birds and mammals preparing for migration or for winter survival. There is always more than enough for both. The unconsumed seeds and fruits are equipped to initiate a new generation of plants come spring.

Enjoy the brief displays of color, and then catalogue the presence of the varied natural pantries that remain. Wildlife will patronize them through the winter.

Autumn should be observed with the understanding that all of its messages are prophetic because its productivity helps to determine what will be possible in days to come. The engine of the growing season has been operating for many months without servicing. Now it must be fueled and winterized so that it will be ready when spring requires it to fire again.

September's Bittersweet Conversation

In my dialogue with the seasons, I'll confess to some difficulty in my conversations with September. September has a beauty and substance not equaled by many months, but it is the first month that seems to be concerned about its age.

I suspect that this is partly due to its recognition that, as with the year itself, it signals the three-quarter point of the growing season. There are many endpoints and very few true starts in September. September is the dance-hall floozy, painted to disguise her age, eager to reminisce and reluctant to discuss the future. I use this comparison, even though I know it is dated, because it is so familiar and I think so appropriate.

This was emphasized in a recent article by Greg Smith in *Beaver Tales*, the newsletter of Beaver Lake Nature Center. Greg, one of Central New York's finest naturalists, is gifted with a special ability to communicate events in nature in terms everyone can understand. He was pointing out how Virginia creeper, poison ivy, and wild grape signal by early coloration that their food pantries are open. This is not just a response to the shut down of energy flow within the plant. The plants, he says, are actively signaling their readiness to serve the mounting appetites of fall. That's typical of September's rhetoric. Many plants begin to signal their last productive act of the season through their own color changes or, more often, through the brightening of the fruit.

In the animal world, too, we see multiple changes of adornment

First aired on WRVO-FM, Sept. 2, 1994.

and of lifestyle. By September, a complete change of clothes has occurred in the male tanager, bobolink, and indigo bunting and a gradual return of nuptial color to the drake waterfowl. Brilliant red, pink, orange, or deep blue infuse the fruits of many shrubs. The heads of grasses, weeds, and many crops turn to gold or brown. Bluebirds, blackbirds, robins, and doves begin to flock, and waterfowl indulge in grand annual conventions from which some of them will not emerge until next April or May.

Grouse and turkey begin to congregate, the grouse in hedgerows and shrubby areas where the last foliage to emerge remains succulent, while the turkey goes to places where early acorns, hickory nuts, and beechnuts have begun to accumulate on the ground. In the days of the passenger pigeon, the turkey might have found formidable competition in the vacuum cleaner feeding of the great doves, but that was a situation too ancient for even the oldest of us to remember today. Today, the turkey's competition mostly has four legs and fur.

Some of September's strongest announcements, however, are hardly news. They have been developing for some time, but who notices green fruit or the breaking down of territorial allegiances in July and August? August does proclaim the event, but only the most sensitive ears are attuned to its quiet statement. In September, these

Bluebirds, blackbirds, robins, and doves begin to flock.

things can no longer be ignored. August gives us warning. September tells us that it all is happening.

Some of you may be saying, "It sounds to me like you are talking about October." There is merit in that thought, but by October our senses have been conditioned. There is a lowered sense of foreboding and a heightened concentration on making the most of what is left. There is still a bit of drama left, but the intensity is just not there. Halloween and even Thanksgiving are on our minds in October, and not in September.

I know it's time to discuss what is bittersweet in all this September talk of productivity and color. I hinted at it when I reminded you that September celebrates very few true starts. September's dialogue is like the ending of a sermon. What it is saying in effect is this: "For my last point before the benediction I offer you the following. Every day the light of one more flower is turned out in the calico fields. The flowers have completed their mission; now it is time for fruits and seeds to mature." Finally, September says, "I'd like to close with a fond benediction on the growing season, but that benediction is really the business of October."

What could be more bittersweet than that?

Twin Miracles of Flight and Frenzy

Part of the secret of a lifetime preoccupation with nature is the ability to find joy and mystery in annually repeated events. Bolstered by a certain amount of past experiences that help to focus the attention, we can settle down assured of accustomed rewards and can search for the unexpected occurrence that makes each episode unique. It's like attending a performance night after night in which a percent of the dialogue is ad libbed.

Right now the robins, waxwings, catbirds, and flickers are energized by the ripening of fruits—cherries in particular and certain others endowed by botanists with such tags as Prunus, Cornus, Lonicera, and Viburnum. Not that the robin is ever really sedate. Apparently losing his cool is part and parcel of the nesting behavior of the male robin. Robins have been known to harass rabbits, chipmunks, and even rock doves who crossed the magic line, the unwritten but real boundary of proximity to the nest.

Still, from August to November, consequent with the ripening of cherry and berry, moments of mass hysteria set in that can produce great theater. We presume, spurred on by our inability to communicate with the source, that this feeding frenzy is serious business, designed to produce fat needed for migration. The evidence is not all circumstantial, but the robin, in assaying this annual mission, expends such prodigious amounts of energy that it calls the whole process into question. You can be forgiven for wondering how there can be any net gain to the robin.

First aired on WRVO-FM, Aug. 27, 1993.

Just this last week I watched a small flock of robins assaulting the wild cherry trees that fringe the suburban gardens at Baltimore Woods. I tried to concentrate on one robin but found it impossible in the frenetic interplay before me. Robins feed and fly in every direction as if each fruit-laden twig is a jet launch pad. They weave in and out as if possessed, sometimes interacting with others, sometimes in solo flight. Others have called this colorful action a bacchanal, sighting tipsiness and other strange behavior. I've seen such episodes, but I don't think they characterize this annual harvest of fruit. It isn't always so frenetic. I've observed some pretty serious banquets in the honeysuckles in my back half acre. They stretched on for several days, the robins harvesting every translucent red berry.

Still, when I sat beneath a mountain ash tree, fitted with camera, telephoto lens, and plenty of film, I found it impossible to capture even a hint of the drama before me. When you focus on one bird in the crowd, you end up with a distracting amount of blurred, undefinable missile activity. At wider angle, shadows tend to consume much of the detail.

It has to be left to the artist, either with pen or brush, to capture the action. Even then it's not easy, but I think that British artist Basil Ede did it justice. I've tried to portray it too, but I lack the skill to produce drama with color and line.

As I watched this week's performance, I discovered at least a half dozen other birds, attracted perhaps by the action or by the perceived safety in numbers. There were three catbirds, two flickers, and an ever changing number of waxwings, apparently through with nesting. They are all somewhat more sedate than the robins, and I wonder if they don't find a certain protection in the bowels of this seething mass. It's easy to be inconspicuous and feed quietly behind the curtain of mass confusion.

On the other hand, there may be an element of safety for the robins in this wild scene. After all, meal time is a time of exposure for any prey species. It's pretty difficult to concentrate on feeding and flight at the same time.

Similarly, successful predation depends on isolation of and concentration on the object of the chase. There might be an element of studied distraction in this seemingly undisciplined ritual. Don't hold me to that. It's just speculation, but in all my observation of feeding robins, bluebirds, and thrushes I've observed little if any predation. You'd expect the birds of prey to be more than normally attracted to such a concentration of potential meals.

What I like about these great avian banquets is their sheer energy and the fact that they are rituals without order, departures from normal behavior, a kind of letting down of the feathers. It's not necessary to develop a deep understanding. Anyone who appreciates the twin miracles of flight and frenzy can find nourishment there, too.

The Story of the Golden Meadows

Early September is a good time to make an annual assessment of the health of agriculture in an area. A good yardstick for that assessment is the amount of gold in the distant landscape. In September, you don't have to be close to a field to judge its agricultural state. The corn is still green, its rows still traced by lines of lighter-colored tassels. Wheat fields have been recently fitted and are mostly brown. They will soon turn to a lively green similar to the putting surfaces on well-tended golf courses. We may be at a loss sometimes to assess the condition of distant pastures or hay fields, but it's a good bet that, except for the fields of birdfoot trefoil, they won't be a golden yellow hue.

No one can doubt that these bright sunny seas of goldenrod, sometimes punctuated by islets of asters, have not known plow, mower, or grazing cattle for a number of years. Such a field is an abandoned field, fast approaching the point where a return to agriculture is most unlikely. The islets of aster will soon be replaced by the spreading domes of dogwood and honeysuckle. Farmers lament this, sensing an exodus of a way of life they hold dear, and understanding that resurrection of the field, as they view it, will soon be out of the question.

The naturalist who esteems wilderness almost as much as life eagerly anticipates the era of the shrubs and even later the time of the forest, but he or she seldom ventures into the golden meadow, apparently unsure of anything of interest in this shoulder-deep hard-

First aired on WRVO-FM, Sept. 10, 1993.

to-wade expanse. Too bad, for there is a great circus of life in this perennial weed patch. Every head of goldenrod is a rallying point for hoards of life: some of it bizarre, some of it artfully concealed, and some supremely beautiful. I first learned of this invertebrate supermarket in my high school days through an article in a nature magazine that documented the congregation of a dozen or more species of insects in one head of Canada goldenrod.

More recently Dick Fischer, one of the deans of American natural history, wrote a fine article for the *Conservationist Magazine* in which he describes some of that life and tells what it is doing there in the goldenrod meadow. I can't help but comment here how much my own life has been blessed by the presence of Dick Fischer. Dick is one of a kind, a scholar with the common touch. Enormously talented himself, he never seems to miss an opportunity to give a colleague a boost. His writings for the general public always have a bit of wit and a lot of information.

I don't know where I got the idea, but one trick I used in teacher workshops and with students was to have them place a medium-sized clear plastic bag over a goldenrod head, gather and tie it at the stem, and shake gently to see what could be found hiding within. With few exceptions, my explorers turned out the bizarre little ambush bug, an oddly constructed true bug designed to mimic the colors and patterns within the goldenrod head. Superbly camouflaged, this powerful but diminutive creature lies in wait to seize unwitting prey. Another interesting hunter, of eight rather than six legs, is the crab spider, a small spider about twice the size of a goldenrod floweret with a bulbous abdomen and large crablike front legs. The better to seize you with, my dear. His mission is similar to that of the ambush bug.

Often my students were surprised to shake out an aphid or two. On closer examination, they'd frequently find a whole herd of these tiny creatures clinging to the goldenrod stem. A related discovery was that of the aphid lion, the larva of the ladybug (ladybird beetle). This larva, along with its adult relatives, is the scourge of the aphid world. Also, where you find aphids, you usually find ants. I've often wondered at the amazing instincts that lead the ant over ground to seek out and climb the stems of these floral skyscrapers, which for them would dwarf the Empire State Building.

In this goldenrod head exercise, I always cautioned my students to observe carefully as they approached their target to see what larger, less camouflaged life they might observe. The goldenrod is the pollen and nectar bonanza of the late growing season, and butterflies, bees, wasps, and occasionally even migrating insect-seeking warblers find them irresistible.

Believe me, it's worth a trip to the golden seacoast to find this bounty and to learn how intricate the interweaving communities of the perennial meadow can be.

An Autumn Less Than Grand Glorious

One of the great traditional events of nature hereabouts has just about run its course for this year. What remains is just a shadow, merely a pale reflection of the peak. I am referring to fall colors, of course: that grand pyrotechnic display by which nature reminds us each year that the growing season, the season of productivity, is over. We will have to survive for nearly half a year on the products of the season.

All around us is evidence of that productivity. Robins and blackbirds by the thousands forage in fields or woodlands. Great flocks of geese and other waterfowl work the sloughs and cornfields. Rabbits of all sizes demonstrate a late-season fondness for the still green remnants of our garden. Mostly hidden from sight but still evident by signs they have left are hoards of meadow voles and deer mice. Last but not least, lest we forget, there are piles of leaves in our dooryards.

When it comes to fall colors, at least in our immediate vicinity, this autumn was not one that my dear departed mother would have called "grand glorious." To her every season, no matter what—and in fact every sunrise—was glorious. Grand glorious was reserved, however, for better times than this presently departing season. There are, of course, good reasons for this assessment, some of which I believe I comprehend and therefore will attempt to share.

The secrets of fall coloration are locked up deep within the cells of the leaves and they are, indeed, reflective of nutritional cycles within the plant. Consider the leaf for a minute. It is often referred to as the

First aired on WRVO-FM, Oct. 24, 1986.

production unit, the manufacturing factory of the plant. The agents of production are plant pigments, chiefly chlorophyll, and sunlight, the energy source. Through their interaction, water, carbon dioxide, and certain other chemical elements are combined to manufacture carbohydrates, the life-giving, energy-yielding base of plant growth.

In order for all this to occur, however, there has to be an orderly flow of raw materials in and manufactured nutrients out of the leaf and into the tree proper. This movement is aided by an elaborate internal plumbing system that connects the leaf with the tree.

As the growing season wanes, layers of cells at the base of the leaf stem, where it attaches to the tree, begin to weaken and to seal off the internal plumbing system. It's as if the pipes in your house or the arteries that feed your heart had become clogged and the flow of water or blood had almost stopped. From the standpoint of the tree, this sealing off prevents moisture loss from the tree following the separation of the leaves. The layer of cells is called the abscission layer. Abscission means cutting away, and it is at this layer that the leaves separate from the tree.

What does all this have to do with fall coloration? Well, chlorophyll, the green coloring matter of the plant contained in tiny packages within the cells of the leaves, is dominant throughout the growing season. With the great reduction in the flow of nutrients, chlorophyll production slows, then ceases. The chlorophyll dissipates rapidly, unveiling yellow, gold, and orange pigments that were present with the chlorophyll but masked by its strong green.

All of these events occur every fall, regardless of the weather, producing what Mother called a glorious glow. The scarlets, purples, and maroons, those deep colors required for a grand-glorious fall depend on an additional chemical reaction. Through this reaction, anthocyanin is produced. Its synthesis is dependent on the amount of sugar trapped in the leaf at the end of the growing season and apparently also is abetted by bright sunlight and a sudden drop in temperature. For the reds, purples, and maroons to be produced abundantly, we need bright days at the end of the growing season along with cold nights.

Observing Autumn

We had a pretty drizzly, dreary September, so none of the conditions required for brilliant fall colors were present and anthocyanin production was low. And that's about it. Golds and yellows are present in the leaf all year, and because they dissipate much more slowly than chlorophyll, we get to see them every season. A bright late summer and a bright cold autumn produce the fiery colors we enjoy so much.

All of these bright colors soon disappear after a brisk fall wind or a heavy rain breaks the abscission layer, and gravity deposits the leaves in windrow piles in our yard. We will have to wait a full year before we'll get a chance to see the anthocyanins again.

The Ebbing Tide of Migration

North America is on the move. That's a statement I can make every year at this time. It's a semiannual event that has been going on at least since the time of the last glacial retreat. Actually, it is a global phenomenon, including both northern and southern hemispheres.

We're talking about migration, of course. The total dynamics of the phenomenon are of mega proportions, but except for a few animated reactions to geese flying overhead, we tend to take the whole thing as a matter of course. Since geese are prospering in a new-found accommodation to the institutions of man, including urban parks and golf courses, few seem to see any disturbing trends in bird populations.

Geese may not be migrating with the same fervor they once did, but they are still amassing in great numbers and visibly and audibly moving between still waters and crop fields. As one of my friends said last year, "The Canadas seem to be going crazy. They don't seem to know which way to fly. I've seen flocks flying north in winter."

Canada geese, despite their reputation, make up a small proportion of the total phenomenon of migration. Migrants of all sizes funnel from all parts of the continent into six well-recognized flyways from Atlantic to Pacific. In the main, their northward migration each spring is a dispersal, a movement from restricted winter quarters to much-expanded nesting ranges. During the nesting season, most species resist crowding. The territorial habits of male or female, or both, help to orchestrate the dispersal.

First aired on WRVO-FM, Sept. 17, 1993.

The fall movement is quite the opposite. The migrants, augmented in numbers by the young of the season, tend to become tolerant of each other, even actively seeking the company of their own kind in preparation for this movement southward. These behavioral changes make such good sense to us that we don't tend to question how this could all occur, how instinct could accommodate such categorical swings in behavior.

It adds nothing to our understanding of the phenomenon to realize that the hallmark migrator of all time, the now extinct passenger pigeon, seems not to have followed that pattern. They were as concentrated in their nesting ground as in their wintering.

Few of us doubt, though not one alive today has seen it at its zenith, that these pigeons were numbered in the billions in their heyday. In their legendary migrations, this living wind, as Leopold tagged them, obscured the sun. It required hours, even days, for a single flock to pass a given spot. Alexander Wilson estimated the numbers in one flock he observed at over a trillion birds. Audubon described an even larger flock. His numbers seem to be extrapolations of Wilson's estimate. One observer described their feeding operation as devastating to the forest floor.

Still, these birds were colonial nesters. Their rookeries covered dozens of square miles each, and, although we have graphic descriptions of conditions within a rookery, we don't seem to know what effect these huge biological juggernauts had on other birdlife in the region. To what extent could grouse and mast-eating songbirds abide the competition from the pigeons? It would take a particularly rich and diverse environment to accommodate both pigeon and other vegetarian birdlife. The ancient hardwood forests of North America may have been that rich, but the agricultural aspirations of the European invaders soon changed the face of the land. It was that great living appetite of the passenger pigeon hordes that yielded, not the scattered and seemingly helpless songbirds. Quietly the meek persisted.

Today as we contemplate the fall migrations, we can begin to draw a parallel with the pigeon, whose Achilles heel was its summer habitat. What ornithologists are now calling the neotropical songbirds are seeing the converse of this old extinction equation. For the songbirds, who can accommodate many changes in their summer habitat, their Achilles heel is their wintering zone, especially for those who go to the rainforests in Central and South America. Researchers are advancing the notion that changes in summering grounds are compounding the problem, but in my observations of land-use patterns, I believe that effect to be temporary. We are still in a cycle of massive land abandonment hereabouts.

However, the devastation of the wintering grounds has already worked its tyranny. Each year the tide of fall migration ebbs a little more, and we seem little more concerned about it than our forefathers were with the disappearance of the pigeon and the bison.

The Monarch

Our Most Unusual Migrant

The fall migration is on. I'm not referring here to bird migration, which most people know about, but to insect migration, which, I think it's safe to say, is known to few. Most people are aware that migration is a response to seasonal change by creatures unable to handle the exigencies of winter in the northeast.

Insects not equipped with an internal heating system or an insulative body covering have had to develop appropriate responses. Some simply perish, leaving behind an ample species-sustaining egg supply. Others spin cocoons or otherwise strategically position their immature stages to quietly weather the winter.

A few, like the mourning cloak butterfly or cluster fly, actually hibernate. But one, the burnt-orange-and-black monarch butterfly, actually undertakes a long desultory migration to the highlands of Mexico or the environs of Monterey Bay in California. The destination depends upon its origin, east or west of the Rockies.

This is a stupendous accomplishment when you think of it. Watch a monarch flitting among the milkweed patches in the back lot and try to imagine it flying 1,700 or 1,800 miles to wintering grounds. Think of such an apparently frail creature braving rainstorm and windstorm to cross all these miles!

Where in the whole of its small body and minuscule brain is the site of computerized information that allows the monarch, just once

First aired on WRVO-FM, Sept. 6, 1985.

Watch the monarch flitting about in the back lot and try to imagine it flying 1,700 miles to wintering grounds.

in its life, to make this long flight and locate its precise wintering ground? Where in this brittle body is the strength and the energy reserve required? To anyone not steeped in the answer-seeking bias of science, it smacks powerfully of miracle. Science, however, is seeking and finding answers.

I first became aware of the research in 1958 when a biology student brought me a dead monarch that she had found on the beach right in front of the Lakeside Dining Hall at Oswego State. To the wing of the monarch had been affixed a tissue-thin tag upon which appeared a number and the cryptic message, "Send to Zoology, U. of Toronto Canada." I did as instructed and in due time received a reply from Norah Urquhart, wife of Fred A. Urquhart who had been studying monarch biology since 1937.

Included in her letter was information about our butterfly along with a brochure explaining Dr. Urquhart's studies and adding interesting information such as the statement, "While some monarchs may make the trip from Canada to Mexico and back, others reproduce and die in the southern U.S. and are replaced in Canadian breeding grounds by their offspring. This further complicates the mystery of the migration, since one or more generations might intervene between the southward migration of the butterfly and the offspring which replace it in the land of its northern birth."

What is the mechanism by which migration information—the

trip-tick, so to speak—is transmitted to future generations? If the monarch outlived its first migration experience, we might inject the factor of tradition—learned response—postulated by some students of bird migration. Urquhart's studies indicate the insect lives for one year, and that suggests that each trip is a maiden voyage. Therefore there is no opportunity to learn from forerunners and forebears. The knowledge of whether migration is truly an individual or a population phenomenon still eludes us, I believe. *Instinct* was Dr. Urquhart's solution, delivered in typically terse style in 1958. At this point, I am unaware of what Dr. Urquhart and his legion of colleagues have discovered since that date.

I don't have to know, for this brief commentary is the response to accounts by friends of observing the congregation of hundreds of monarchs along the eastern shores of Lake Ontario this September weekend. This reminded me of an article by Dr. Urquhart in an earlier issue of *National Geographic* reporting the discovery of the wintering grounds, for monarchs spawned in the eastern United States, in the Sierra Madre Mountains of Mexico. In that article were photos in which the ground and the evergreens were turned a rusty brown by hoards of hibernating monarchs. That reminded me of another article about Pacific Grove California, the wintering ground of all monarchs spawned west of the Rockies. Pacific Grove has an annual celebration to mark the return of the monarchs. They have passed strict laws to protect the wintering hoards.

The details of monarch migration are still only partly known. Who can tell what life secrets will be unlocked by the study of these mysteries. Meanwhile, it is significant to note that we have learned more that is useful from this insect than from all the billions of passenger pigeons we destroyed before we got a chance to study them.

The Loon

Sometimes forceful events that affect the common lifestyle and the common value system also produce ripples that either harm or benefit causes far removed from the mainstream. Recent events in my own life have pointed out such a situation even though I missed the forceful event and for a long time was unable to understand the by-product. I'll explain.

The common loon, one of the handsomest and most unusual of our native waterfowl, has been in a struggle for survival. The loon's well-being, along with that of the brook trout, is apparently a bellwether of changing conditions in lakes of the northern United States and Canada. A major factor in this change may be the result of acid fallout from storms, what we call acid rain.

The decrease of the loon was not noted quite as soon as was the decrease in brook and lake trout. It took a while for the deleterious effects of acid rain to work their way up the food chain, but it stands to reason that anything that destroys aquatic life is eventually going to harm those creatures that feed on that life.

Because it was an obscure and mysterious bird, the plight of the loon went unnoticed until the movie *On Golden Pond* brought it to the attention of the mainstream. Suddenly people began to notice that the loon was indeed a handsome bird, a bird with mystique. Somehow this bird became symbolic of an appealing human situation.

Although I did not see the film at that time, I soon became aware of the interest in loons: paintings, notepaper, articles in the mass

First aired on WRVO-FM, Oct. 18, 1991.

media, organizations that took the loon for their logo or even for their mascot. People began to ask me if I had ever painted a loon, or if I had any loon notepaper, or if I was interested in doing loon carvings.

Most interesting to me was the fact that organizations for the protection of the loon began to grow. The cause of the loon's plight, it appears, is more complex than just acid rain, but it is possible that its lingering popularity is going to be helpful to it.

We see loons regularly on Central New York's lakes and waterways during the winter months. These distant views of two-toned gray-brown and white birds swimming singly or in small groups, diving and occasionally skittering across the water in a ponderous low-level takeoff are but a shadow of the loon at home in some Adirondack lake. There, it isn't just its sartorial splendor but also its voice that you remember. I recall a foggy morning on Raquette Lake when the wild voice of the loon preceded its emergence from fog within a stone's throw of my vantage point. Both events were hair raising and memorable to a budding naturalist.

Loon nests are often quite exposed, a pile of rotting vegetation right on the shoreline or mounded up in a marshy bay. The usual complement of eggs is two, but a lone egg is common and three occasional. Loon watchers have reported to me that normally only one egg hatches and that loons rarely raise more than one chick. The dark fuzzy chicks, which hatch after twenty-six to twenty-eight days of incubation, are soon able to swim and dive. They frequently climb upon the back of the adult, sedately riding about.

The few views I've seen of the lone chick with the adults have made it look rather forlorn, but they seem to thrive in those remote settings. By fall they are feathered and able to fly, and it won't be long before we'll begin to see a few of them diving for minnows and other aquatic life in lakes or larger waterways. As their preferred haunts freeze over, they retreat only as far southward as is necessary to find open water. This is when we see them in Central New York.

I realize this is a sketchy profile of an interesting bird. For now, perhaps, we can be satisfied to ponder the situation the loon represents. An obscure bird that has been victimized by the actions of man

It isn't just the loon's sartorial splendor but also its voice that you remember.

is hardly valued, its demise hardly lamented. When suddenly it springs to attention and gains our affection, we have a new perspective. Something we value is being taken from us. Such compassion is all to the good. What I lament is the fact that it takes such an event to highlight the folly of unchecked environmental contamination. Remember, even though it takes a while to work their way up the food chains, these follies soon reach us one way or another.

In Search of the Gobbler's Tale

He's as American as pumpkin pie and maize and at times as elegant as any North American. John James Audubon made him the subject of his most celebrated portrait, and Benjamin Franklin fervently advocated him for our national symbol instead of the eagle. He has been variously described as the stupidest, the wariest, and the most intelligent of game birds. For the pioneer, who found it essential to learn his ways, he provided one of the most satisfactory and dependable meat sources that the eastern forests could afford.

Venerated by Native American and settler alike, the wild turkey had in him the stuff of which legends are made, but like many other legendary Americans, from towering chestnut tree to lowering mountain lion, he yielded to the axe, the gun, and the exotic diseases of the European. New York's loss of the turkey went hand in hand with its loss of the ancient forests, for the turkey was always a creature of the oak, beech, and chestnut ridges and of the forest glade. Such names as Turkey Hill, Tom Mountain, Gobbler's Knob, and Turkey Hollow that mark our neighborhoods remain to celebrate these last bastions in the increasingly woodless countryside of the last century.

Today we classify him in more prosaic terms as an example of forest wildlife, and we can hail him as a native returned. The big woods of southern New York once again resound to his raucous gobble and answering "pee-ok." Those who have observed him in the wild have found him to be, as they say, quite a piece of work.

Originally published in the *Baldwinsville Messenger*, Nov. 27, 1974. First aired on WRVO-FM, Nov. 27, 1992.

The turkey is a member of the grouse and pheasant clan, which makes him a near relative of the peacock and a distant relative of the chicken. Like other members of this small group of bird families, he is polygamous. This means he collects a harem of hens who he vigorously defends against interloping toms. He is well endowed for this defense with formidable spurs, brightly colored expandable snood and wattles, stiff erectile plumage, and a tail as big as the top of a bushel basket.

These last attributes, including the gobbler's tail, are important to impress his rivals and his consorts. Picture him in the center of a forest glade, his elegant tail spread like an Indian war bonnet, his burnished copper plumage standing on end, and the fleshy wattles on face and neck engorged with blood and showing a brilliant red and blue. He looks twice as big as life, as pompous as a lord. Standing there stiff-legged and expansive, he lowers his head and wings and performs a mincing two-step while shaking his plumes with an impressive rattle. He turns slowly from left to right, occasionally uttering a strident "gobble-obble-obble."

At a sign of danger, he may deflate like a punctured balloon, pomp and circumstance apparently forgotten, and melt silently into the woodland shadows. The stuff of which legends are made, indeed! When danger does not threaten, the performance may go on for some time, its courtly fashion an example of the visual language of courtship and mating.

The slim, comparatively drab hen is much smaller than the gobbler, eight to ten pounds as compared to fifteen to twenty in the male. For nesting, she seeks a spot at the base of a bastioned oak where shrubs and herbs provide screening cover but do not obscure the view. The ten to twelve eggs, about the color of dried leaves with darker splotches, are half again as big as a jumbo chicken's egg. They are placed in a leaf-lined depression and faithfully incubated for four full weeks. The youngsters are able to run about in search of food soon after hatching. The hen shepherds her brood throughout the winter. However, the gobbler has nothing to do with all these domesticities. Chauvinism is typified by, and may have originated with, the members of the pheasant-peacock-turkey tribes.

The poults require a high percentage of protein, as do many young birds. For that reason, insects are an important part of the first summer's diet. The young turkeys grow rapidly and are able to join the adult in treetop roosts by the time they are a month old. By fall, they are vest-pocket editions of the adults, but the male requires two years to reach full maturity.

Turkeys walk great distances, covering miles daily in search of acorns and other mast. My limited experience with turkeys in the wild indicates that they are difficult to flush. Except for one time near Ithaca, when I spooked several roosting in a pine, I have always seen them on the ground. The wingspan averages nearly five feet, so when you do flush them, it is a memorable experience.

The wild turkey has returned to New York through the combined efforts of farmers who abandoned so much land in Depression times and the biologists of the Conservation Department who imported brood stock and eggs, and reared young birds for liberation into favorable habitat.

The story of turkey propagation is an interesting one, about which many tales are told at Sherburne. It was there, when the

One time I spooked several turkeys roosting in a pine.

Rogers Center was a game farm, that the bulk of the birds were reared. Suffice to say that the propagation unit encountered all the problems that beset the domestic turkey raiser, plus a few based on traits that the turkey lost in the process of domestication.

In this season, when we enjoy a helping of super-turkey at our holiday table, we may pause to think about a native returned, a rare opportunity in this era when so many of our natives have shown us their tail for the last time.

November's Dialogue

When it comes to easy dialogue between the natural world and man, November is the first in a series of months when the information flow is at low tide. Of course, we do talk about the weather, with little positive to say about that. And we do pause briefly at Thanksgiving and Christmas to celebrate nature's bounty through food and festive decoration. I know, however, that most people will turn their backs on the wild world as soon as they have disposed of the fallen leaves from their dooryards.

Actually, November, noted for its bleakness and damp austerity, may be one of the most talkative of months if we can but learn the language. In November, nature offers the solution to many of the mysteries it has been nurturing throughout the growing season. Step forth with me on a brisk November morning and we'll seek out the gossip of the season.

The grass, still whitened and stiffened with frost in shaded patches, grows vibrant and supple as soon as the warming rays of the sun can reach it. Our lawn grasses provide lessons in adaptability. Ever green and ever growing, most of the grass species in our lawns are aliens selected for just those qualities. Most of our native grasses are slower to green and quicker to brown.

Perhaps the first bit of nature's conversation in November is this: Whatever the warming effect of the sun during the day, there is always the night, and in November that is a time of extreme cooling. The brighter the day and the warmer the sun, the greater the radia-

Originally published in the *Baldwinsville Messenger*, Nov. 8, 1978.

tive heat loss at night. Those plants and animals that are not adapted to extreme nighttime cooling will have to make other arrangements by November. That may be the subject matter of the second of November's conversations. What are these other arrangements?

Completely surrounding the tomato patch, now planted to winter rye, is a fringe of weeds and grasses, already brown and shrivelled. Upon examination, lamb's quarters, amaranth, and ragweed prove to be heavily laden with ripe seeds, waiting for tree sparrows and juncos to find them. It is the fate of the annual weeds that, no matter how spectacular their growth during the summer, the entire future of their race is wrapped up in a handful of seeds for the production of which they have literally given their all. The hazards are many.

In this season, weed patches become lunch counters for all manner of sparrows and finches, many of which use our fields as way stations on their southward migration. The field-edge lunch counter is open throughout the winter, snow permitting, but there is always a surplus of seeds from which next year's crop will spring. What a magnificent gamble!

So far we have solved no mysteries, just indulged in straightforward dialogue, but if we direct our attention to the shrubfield and woodlands, we will begin to discover little mysteries revealed. As we mosey down the lane, an inch-thick mat of leaves crunches underfoot. They are rapidly losing the xanthophyll and anthocyanin that imparted the brilliant golds and reds to the October foliage. Beside that shining array, November woodlands may look bleak and uninviting.

Let's make sure, however, that we don't miss the flaming clusters of mountain ash and hawthorn, which are not even visible until their leaves have disappeared. I am particularly fond of the hawthorns. Worldwide there are some 1,300 species in all sizes and shapes. In some the red fruit is the size of a pea, in others it is the size of a small apple. Not all bear red fruits. It is the general acceptance of these fruit by grouse, pheasant, deer, cottontail, and various songbirds that interests me most.

If I watch the thorn apple long enough, I may see many wildlife dramas. I will also find, if I examine the close-knit branches, the answers to questions I have been harboring since mid-summer. See! The catbird that greeted my daily passage with protest did place his nest among the green fruits. Nearer the ground is the remains of the chestnut-sided warbler's nest. All the time I had placed him over in the middle of that blackberry thicket. Well, what do you know, the blackberry thicket holds the yellow-throat's nest. Thus are summer's mysteries solved in November.

As we wander along, we may find the oriole's nest high up in a black cherry, the vireo's nest in the lower branches of a beech tree, a crow's nest high up in a red oak, and so on. The number of birds that greeted my daily summer sojourns presaged this density of nesting. "All that is past history," you may say. Yes, but along with the expected, I make many unexpected finds: a redstart's nest where I had seen no redstarts all summer, a grosbeak's nest within a few feet of my daily passage. He sneaked that one in on me.

The importance of November's dialogue may not rest in its confirmations of last summer's observations but in its predictions of next summer's events. I'll keep my eyes open for redstart and grosbeak next summer, and if the law of averages holds, I'll find some new reward.

Observing Winter

There is a power in the sun rays and the rising of the sun. There is a magic that envelopes those early hours of rising, somehow instilling everything with a feeling of beginning, of happiness. I don't think that I've ever watched a sunrise without experiencing a rising of new joy starting at my feet, and washing upwards till it burst out from my crown chakra like a flower. —JWD

Winter is the period of rest and recuperation for the wild community. It starts with the falling of leaves and fruit, and with the frantic activity of many wild creatures to prepare for escape or for a profound alteration of lifestyle. Many will have completely changed their plumage or pelage to provide both an undercoat of down or soft fur and an overcoat of coarser material. A layer of fat will provide both insulation and assurance of survival for periods when food is scarce.

The hoards of insects will have completely disappeared, a few to hibernate, but most having left behind only eggs or properly protected immatures to repopulate the next growing season. Snow provides a great insulative counterpane that, despite its icy substance, helps to make up for the loss of green cover.

Winter's engine may appear to be in idle, but anyone who goes to the winter woods or fields finds a richness of life, some of it the more evident because of the starkness of the landscape.

The way to observe the winter woods is to visit the catalogue of nature's pantry you made in late autumn in search of wildlife that has no other choice but to visit these diners with frequency. While you are there, look carefully for the sleeping embryo of spring.

The Texture of Winter

During my time as a Conservation Department biologist and later as a biology teacher at Oswego State, I had more than passing acquaintance with a group of math-science-inclined people properly called biostatisticians. As a group they seemed committed to the discovery of new and more meaningful measures of the ebb and flow of life.

It was one of their fraternity who discovered that the fortunes of the Canada lynx were directly related to the fortunes of the varying and arctic hares, just by examining the fur harvest records of the Hudson's Bay Company. Another researcher discovered that the hare's numbers were cyclic with ten-year peaks and valleys.

Biostatisticians can also tell us many things about the statistical dimensions of winter, but somehow dry figures miss the essence of the season. Perhaps statisticians just measure the wrong things. More likely, I think, is that the essence of winter is more in its texture than in its dimensions.

Biologically, winter is the nadir, the low point, demanding enormous energy output but returning the minimum of life support. Its numbers are all too discouraging. Wild food reserves dwindle every day. Temperatures drop. Populations wane as the life curve drops toward the low point.

A winter walk, however, is a most rewarding thing. The heart pumps, the pulses quicken, and the vital juices flow. The colors are drab and cold, but wind and sun working on the medium of snow sculpt and reshape the landscape in a most comely fashion. Scars

Originally published in the *Baldwinsville Messenger*, Feb. 11, 1976; first aired on WRVO-FM, Jan. 3, 1986.

The hare's numbers are cyclic with ten-year peaks and valleys.

and gashes disappear; even the hard-edged geometric forms of man's design are softened and rounded. Any bit of color stands out. Against the snow a cardinal becomes a bird of fire, a blue jay a fluttering bit of heaven.

"Don't romanticize," you say. "For me winter is all cold and snow and aching sacroiliacs." Even the hardship has its point that these people miss. In winter we are never at a loss for conversation, and the more impressive the stats, the freer the word flow. The great snows and blizzards of the past have always had a temporary humanizing effect on their victims no matter how unresponsive they may be at other times. Strangers strike up conversations waiting for trains or buses, and otherwise distant neighbors become good friends through shared adversity.

I remember well how the blizzard of 1966, which pinned us down for a week or more, served just that function. We met in groups in various homes, sharing food, information, and even confidences. It was like group therapy. Try to imagine that at any other time.

Another comfort we tend to associate with deep and forbidding winter is that of the hearthside. It's good to warm the soles of the feet as the storm descends. Many were unaware of that pleasure until they installed a standing fireplace or a Franklin stove. Of course, these add-ons often foul up well-designed central heating systems, and they have made a good split of oak as scarce and expensive as a good lamb chop. However, it does something for the soul that a person like me who grew up in a house with four fireplaces can tell you has ancient roots.

And then there's that whole business of winter sports. There was a time when the downhill skier, the trapper, and the rabbit hunter had the winter woods pretty much to themselves. Then came the snowmobile. To the snowmobiler, no area is too remote and no hour of the day or night sacred. Now, the cross-country skier has joined the growing throng and his numbers are legion. Even snowshoeing has had a renaissance. All of these people, exquisitely dressed for the weather, are finding in the winter landscape a charm and beauty as rewarding as the exercise.

They are also encountering wildlife with increasing frequency. This may be a bit unsettling to wildlife that has grown accustomed to winter privacy, and, of course, it's important for us to be sensitive to that. But in the main, wildlife will accommodate and people's respect for rights of wildlife should increase with exposure.

Encountering a deer, an ermine, a pileated woodpecker, or a ruffed grouse along the trail provides spice to anyone's outing. When we begin to recognize the subtle signs left by the wildlife and learn to read their messages in the snow, a new dimension is added to our own lives. Built into our growing appreciation of the texture of winter may be a newfound understanding of the dimensions and limitations of the biosphere in which we live and take nourishment.

Then the biostatisticians' cryptic language assumes new meaning, and our increased comprehension of nature's great expanse adds to our appreciation of its essence. That's the purpose of most nature writing, to convert its bewildering details into simple principles we can use in our own lives.

White Shadow of the Woods

Driving along on my way to Oswego recently, I noted a small patch of soiled white fur plastered to the tarvia, apparently by the heavy wheels of a truck. An ignominious end for an interesting and little-known hunter, the weasel. It took me back fifteen years, shortly after we had opened Beaver Lake Nature Center, when an ermine, the winter-color phase of the short-tailed weasel, chose to hunt during daylight hours in the woods adjacent to the building.

Because there was no snow on the ground, his lovely white

First aired on WRVO-FM, Jan. 11, 1991.

An ermine is the winter-color phase of the weasel.

pelage made him conspicuous indeed. Only the black tip of his tail matched his surroundings, and that only in the deepest shadows. This may have placed him at some disadvantage in stalking the small mammals and birds that are his usual fare, and may have accounted for his being abroad in areas where we had not seen him before. Perhaps he had not dined with accustomed regularity since donning his immaculate white coat.

This wraithlike creature is a member of an interesting and mysterious clan of short-legged and mostly slim-bodied hunting machines that includes the fisher or pekan, the marten or sable, the ferret and polecat, the mink and otter. Less weasel-like in appearance and far more formidable in reputation are the skunk, the badger, the ratel, and the wolverine. This last creature, the largest of the land weasels, is considered pound for pound to be the most formidable of North American mammals. Even bear and mountain lion are said to avoid confrontation with it.

The ermine, weighing less than a pound, and measuring less than a foot in length, is a fierce and relentless hunter. Although afraid of humans, the ermine seems possessed of overpowering curiosity, frequently appearing again and again, apparently trying for a better view.

Once when I was sketching from a perch on a huge fallen willow trunk by the banks of the Chenango River, my attention was attracted by a scurrying movement at the far end. One end of the debarked and bleached log lay at the apex of a huge jam of driftwood, and as I carefully shifted my eyes in the direction of the movement, I saw the slim chocolate-brown body of a large New York or long-tailed weasel disappearing into the tangle of sticks. He reappeared in a second and took a few more testing steps in my direction. This kept up for ten minutes, and because I had my camera ready, with telephoto lens attached, I obtained several passable pictures of him. In my excitement, however, I behaved like an amateur and wasted more good opportunities than I took advantage of. It soon became clear that the weasel was determined to use the log as a bridge, so I retreated and allowed him to pass.

Most of my experiences with weasels have proven them to be energetic, curious, and relatively fearless, but not all of them have had such innocuous results. Once, for instance, when I was working at the Ithaca Game Farm, a short-tailed weasel dispatched over five dozen young pheasant chicks between 5:00 P.M. when I checked the birds last and 6:00 P.M. when the night man checked them.

Many would say that this record of ruthless killing was also typical of weasels. Our best guess, however, was that he had come in search of food for his young. Being unable to drag any of the chicks out of the brooder house, he kept killing until he found one that he could squeeze through the tiny cracks and holes in the pen. Nearly every available hole was stuffed with a dead chick, securely lodged there.

In perhaps a dozen encounters with weasels, including observing the killing of deer mice, field mice, and shrews, but never any wild birds, my admiration for their beauty and their efficiency has grown. Weasels have natural enemies including both dogs and house cats, but the most formidable enemy may still be the prejudiced hunter who attempts to wipe out every one he sees.

There's not much sense in persecuting one of our most persistent allies in our never-ending battle against rodents. Every weasel killed may be a hundred field mice saved. One hundred of those prolific rascals saved could mean a million offspring, which could eat tons of clover, alfalfa, and timothy, not to mention wheat, oats, and corn.

If you happen to see a weasel, remember he is an ally in the problem of controlling rats and mice, and therefore, he is worthy of protection.

Feeder Talk

I'm sitting at home today, contemplating a mild snowstorm outside the window. Weather forecasters have indicated that here in Marcellus we are experiencing the fringe of a lake-effect disturbance, one of only two or three legitimate snowstorms we've seen this winter. Such weather makes me think of bird feeders. Perhaps that's because several people have asked me over the holiday season whether it really made any sense to set up a bird feeder when the weather is so open.

Not an easy question to answer, really, because the answer depends upon the point of view. From the standpoint of nature and native birds, there is no real evidence that feeders make any sense at all. Starvation is seldom the thing that brings wild birds down in winter. It is much more often the combination of disease, exposure, and predation that does wildlife in. There is some evidence that feeders may contribute to making birds more vulnerable to both disease and predation by concentrating them unnaturally. This is an insignificant factor, I believe.

Getting back to the question, however: if wild birds don't really need feeders, how come birds flock to them in such big numbers? Answer me that. If somebody set up a self-service gas station offering free gas, would any of us say, "Hey, we've got plenty of gas without that cheap fuel"? No, and neither would the birds pass by feeder fare. It's free fuel. In addition, the lunch counter is usually much more sheltered than many wild food sources. Chalk up two points

First aired on WRVO-FM, Jan. 11, 1985.

For the birds, the feeder provides a cheap, handy food supply.

for the feeder. For the birds, the feeder provides a cheap, handy food supply.

How about the charge made by some biologists that feeders have significantly changed behavior patterns of birds? I think the jury is still out on that one. I've seen no persuasive studies, but I do note how readily birds that flock to a feeder develop, without true strife, an order of feeding that assures everyone a chance at the lunch counter.

I note, for instance, that at Baltimore Woods this winter one particular mourning dove is dominant. When he, or she, is at the feeder, no other bird, neither red-bellied woodpecker nor blue jay, can dislodge it. A pair of red-bellied woodpeckers seems to be next. Blue jays retreat promptly when either red-belly arrives. All of the blue jays seem to come next, although I have seen an occasional instance where one has given way to a nuthatch or a hairy woodpecker. I suspect the same kind of rigmarole occurs at natural food counters such as the sumac copse or the wild grape tangle.

We don't seem to be getting much closer to an answer to the original question, "Do we set up a feeder this year or not?" OK, let's go at it from another standpoint. What makes a good feeder location? And what constitutes a good feeder? That may seem to be beside the point, but just hear me out.

Many people who live in relatively new suburban or inner-city sites have fairly open back yards with little or no screening. These are the poorest sites for feeders, but window shelves on the sheltered side of the house will often have good success. It is also possible right now to collect used Christmas trees. A minimum of four or five can be anchored together with stakes and twine to form good screening for a feeder. Properly located, this artificial copse will provide shelter from wind and handy escape cover from predators. And it should last all winter.

If your property is well provided with shrubs, especially evergreens, you have much more flexibility in location for a feeder. Remember a good view from a favorite window is an important factor, but do be careful to keep the location as secure as possible from cats and dogs. Tree sparrows and juncos will appreciate exposed open shelves near or on the ground and at least two cat leaps away from screening cover.

Regarding foods, I prefer simple fare. Black sunflower seed, cracked corn, niger (some people call it thistle), and suet are all I usually have. Seed mixes including sorghum, millets, and milo are usually money wasters unless you have a large clientele of sparrows and juncos using your feeder. Watch what is happening at your feeder if you use mixes. Occasionally go out and blow away the sunflower hulls and see if the percentage of millet and sorghum left seems very high. If you have the right mix, most of the small seeds will be gone, too. I buy the foods separately and use less than ten pounds of mix to fifty pounds of sunflower, if I use the mix at all.

Another great feeder food is peanuts: whole kernel, peanut hearts, or peanut butter. Expensive but welcome. Use natural peanut butter, the kind that separates. It's best and don't worry about the birds gagging on it. They don't.

There are probably other things I should mention but none come to mind right now. Oh yes! How did I answer the question about setting up a feeder in an open winter? Go ahead. As soon as possible. It will do you all kinds of good. Feeders, you see, are for people, not primarily for birds. If you start a feeder and then abandon it, the birds will go someplace else and find food, but then what will you do to replace the entertainment and beauty?

Feeders are for people. Aren't we lucky that the birds enjoy them too?

The Bald Eagle

When our founding fathers were in the process of selecting a national seal and thereby insuring the identity of our national emblem, there was some controversy about the final selection. It was an August group of men including many of the principles who had earlier drawn up the Declaration of Independence.

The group was chaired by Benjamin Franklin who, although he seems to have approved of the seal, was critical of the selection for the national emblem. The eagle, he averred, was a bird of bad moral character, too lazy to fish for himself and too cowardly to stand in his own territory when attacked by the little kingbird. Franklin's candidate for national emblem appears to have been the wild turkey. Though "a little vain and silly," Franklin said, it was still "a true American and a bird of courage."

Franklin neatly overlooked or apparently did not know that the tom turkey was a bit of a philanderer, a confirmed polygamist, who whenever possible would amass a harem of a half dozen hens or more. Further, he is so busy with his duties as landholder and sire that he has no time or interest, it seems, in the young ones his mates rear.

The eagle, on the other hand, appears to be a confirmed monogamist, and if somewhat less than diligent in defense of the nest against intruders, at least humans, he is faithful in attendance to the needs of mate and offspring. Any judgment as to the relative morality of eagle and turkey is at best a standoff and at worst distinctly favorable to the eagle.

First aired on WRVO-FM, Nov. 24, 1990.

It is also a silly argument. If eagles and turkeys really had moral codes, they'd both fade into oblivion. In nature it's every creature for himself. Get food as you can, even if it means harassing and robbing an osprey. Fight when it seems right, take care of what your instinct directs, but by all odds survive. Any turkey or eagle who could read Deuteronomy 22 would instantly be reassured. The Mosaic Law says protect the breeding stock not the offspring, another somewhat fatuous speculation, however, since no eagle or turkey needs to read the Bible to know how to comport itself.

I've talked about the turkey more than once before, so let's consider the eagle for a minute. An impressive bird, its seven-foot wingspan gives a much more massive appearance than its weight and other dimensions would warrant. Normal weight is about twelve pounds. Both turkey and swan are several times as large.

Eagles build extremely bulky nests, always occupying a major crotch of a large tree anywhere from thirty-five to seventy feet up. The average number of eggs is two. The young hatch after about five weeks of incubation. When hatched, the young are small and covered with down that they exchange for feathers after a month. After another month or month and a half, they are said to be ready to leave the nest but not yet to leave the adults. Both parents are fully involved over this total period of five weeks in the egg and eight to ten weeks in the nest. It is three years before the immature eagle gains its white head and tail and is ready to breed.

The history of our national emblem has been checkered, at best. I can remember observing eagles with some regularity as a youth along the shores of Lake Ontario. I have observed them several times stealing fish from ospreys, a task at which they are truly accomplished, catching the released fish before it touches the ground. I have also observed them feeding on dead carp and on deer carcasses, both of which they visited periodically until everything was gone. Not a pleasant thought for you or me, but obviously okay with the eagle.

Cattle and sheep ranchers are vehement in their condemnation of eagles, which they claim are kill newborn calves and lambs. They use this argument as an excuse for the illegal slaughter of the birds even though the bald eagle is largely a scavenger and fisherman. It seems more likely that they are visiting carcasses killed by some other agent.

The eagle needs and deserves our protection. It is one of our few remaining symbols of a free and unfettered environment.

Reynard!

Red Menace or Worthy Citizen?

Nature bookshelves offer a variety of books on the red fox, an animal whose size is dwarfed by its reputation. The fox is actually a small mammal weighing only from ten to fifteen pounds. It is about three feet in length including that spectacular tail and about fifteen inches in height at the shoulders.

My first awareness of the fox may have come like yours, through Aesop's Fables, Thornton Burgess's Mother Westwind stories, or Uncle Remus. Each one paints a slightly different picture of the fox: sly, devious, rapacious but gullible, and no match for the likes of Brer Rabbit. That summarizes the unreal imagery the fox conjures up in most minds.

Many old sportsmen credit the fox singlehandedly with the decline of the pheasant and the cyclic fluctuations of the rabbit, not to mention grouse. They paint a black picture of the foxes' environmental citizenship. The fox is not really worthy of this reputation. In the first place, its environmental citizenship is much better than we will allow. It does its job: partly predator, partly gleaner, partly scavenger.

The male fox is also an exemplary mate, carrying food for its spouse and helping with the rearing of the young. It is during this period of family responsibility when the fox runs into trouble with the farmer over depredations in the henhouse.

I can't remember the first time I saw a red fox in the wild. Proba-

Originally published in the *Baldwinsville Messenger*, Nov. 29, 1978.

bly in winter when its rich red coat silhouetted against a white snowbank is every bit as spectacular as is a male cardinal in a snow-covered spruce. The fox is a dainty animal, with graceful lines and great speed afoot. Its fine features and its alertness project an impression of intelligence. Fox hunters are full of great tales about its uncanny skills at confounding the hounds.

My own impressions are somewhat different. For one thing, the fox seems to have an inordinate amount of curiosity and perhaps an unhealthy disdain for people. I remember a number of years ago when I was doing some consulting work for the Nassau County Board of Educational Services at Caumsett Park on the North Shore of Long Island. I encountered red foxes everywhere on those acres, denning in culverts, hunting in weedy pastures, even foraging for crayfish or minnows in a small stream. Caumsett was the estate of publisher Marshall Field III. It was abandoned by his widow when she sold it to the state, so there was much incidental history strewn about in some of its amazing buildings.

I was standing one morning in the workroom of the greenhouse complex, thumbing through a calendar in which planting and grounds care schedules were entered, when I happened to look up. There, not ten feet away standing in a planter that brought it to just about eye level, was a beautiful red fox watching me attentively. There was a glass-paneled door between us, but that did little to lessen my reaction. I was startled and amazed. As I looked up, the fox, its curiosity satisfied, turned and ambled away, leaping from planter to planter and exiting the greenhouse through an open door at the far end.

I suspected a den, perhaps secreted under one of the piles of debris, but a careful search turned up none of the typical signs of one. Perhaps the fox's interest in the greenhouse involved mice or chipmunks.

The Caumsett foxes, despite their boldness and curiosity, gave every evidence of excellent health. Still, such concentrations do raise the specter of rabies to anyone my age who remembers one great rabies scare in Central New York immediately following World War II.

152 | Observing Winter

At that time I was a student at Cornell when Tompkins County cows died of rabies, and parents were afraid to allow their children to wander in the fields and woodlands for fear of rabid foxes.

Both Rice Creek and Baltimore Woods today support healthy fox populations, again providing evidence of the foxes' remarkable adjustment to people. In both places, the foxes seem to have an exquisite awareness of human schedules, so the chances of surprising one near the buildings is greatest at times when people are not usually around.

An example of this occurred at Rice Creek several years ago. The day when we switched from daylight savings to standard time left us in the building an hour later than usual according to fox time. At just about 4:10 standard time, 5:10 daylight, a beautiful adult red fox ambled across the lawn and proceeded to hunt the shoreline of the pond, pausing a moment to watch a small group of wigeon feeding

The fox seems to have an inordinate amount of curiosity and perhaps an unhealthy disdain for people.

just offshore. It then continued along the shoreline passing from sight behind a clump of alders. Within a few minutes it returned again, still foraging. Suddenly it leaped into the shoreline sedges, emerging with a mouse. It proceeded to play with the mouse for some time before dispatching it.

Rice Creek director Don Cox and I watched this whole episode from the gallery window, aware that what we were watching was probably habitual behavior for the fox, whose sense of timing made no allowance for such complications as daylight and standard time.

Well, I started out to tell something about the biology and environmental citizenship of the red fox, and ended up writing mostly about its impact on me. That's typical of this animal whose reputation always exceeds his actions.

Happy New Year, Gregorian and Natural

Present day calendars notwithstanding, we're all really sun worshipers. The government may compute our taxes based on the calendar year, but our natural cycles, as distinct from our fiscal cycles, are definitely sun-oriented.

Such things as annual migrations in search of basking conditions, our expeditions to the seed store, the change from rake to snow shovel to spading fork are all much more aligned with solstice and equinox than with any monthly timetables. Our calendars seem to ignore this. The calendar year starts in the middle of winter when we are tired from Christmas preparations and year-end celebrations, and are ready to admit that what we need most to start the new year is two weeks of rest.

What a way to start a new year, resting up from the terminal excesses of the last. Wildlife has a different approach. The horned owl, for instance, triggered perhaps by increasing day length, addresses himself to the reestablishment of the pair bond with his mate. With great dignity and style, he approaches her with courtly gestures all the time showering her with vocal endearments. Not to be outdone, she responds in kind. It is a minipageant of exceeding comeliness. There, my heart tells me, is the way the new year should be celebrated.

January brings the fox and skunk out, too. Make no mistake about it, however, the forces that bring them abroad to salute January are the cumulative effect of several weeks of internal preparations that date from the hibernal equinox.

Originally published in the *Baldwinsville Messenger*, Dec. 29, 1976; first aired on WRVO-FM, Dec. 29, 1990.

The horned owl addresses himself to the reestablishment of the pair bond with his mate.

By now you may be ready to remind me that the Gregorian calendar is actually based on cosmic, or at least solar mathematics. True, and it has served well to keep us free of most confusions, but it is a rigged affair combined of thirty-one, thirty, and twenty-eight day months with an extra day stuck on like a Band-Aid every fourth year to keep the seasons from wandering. However, it buries the great pivotal solunar events in the middle of the third, sixth, ninth, and twelfth months, and endows us with so many different starting dates to worry about that we can't keep them straight.

Ancient man had a different approach. Without all this modern fiscality to worry about, he planted, hunted, worshiped, and perhaps even reproduced to the rhythms of sun and moon. The only problem was to be able to predict the coming events. The ancient Egyptians, for instance, long ago calculated that the solar year was one quarter day longer than 365, and learned to chart its course. Even the much less sophisticated Plains Indians had a means of prediction just recently discovered by a researcher. The strange stone medicine wheels, always presumed to be related to superstition or to mundane ceremony, turn out to be astronomical devices that align perfectly with sunrise and sunset of the equinox, and with other events that relate to the changing solar year. It is perhaps significant that the Indians rapidly lost the ability to use and interpret these devices when brought into constant contact with the European who worshiped and danced to a different set of gods. We transplant effectively the trappings of our own divorcement from the natural world.

In this season however, when we celebrate the coming of the

Prince of Peace, from whose nativity we now reckon all our time, it does seem petty to dwell on fiscal obfuscations of the good life. Better, maybe, just to say, "Merry Christmas and a Happy Gregorian year, with overtones of those natural blessings regulated by equinox and solstice!"

The January–Spring Syndrome

In the main I'm a very conservative person, but I do have a few chronic afflictions that might seem radical to some of you. One of them is the January-spring syndrome, which descends on me every year, sometimes even before the old year has quite run its course. Its basic expression is an inexplicable emotional lift as I greet each advancing January sunrise. I automatically feel better every daybreak in January, regardless of the weather, than I did on any December daybreak, save Christmas, which, to me, is the commemoration of an eternal blessing.

It took science a good many decades to discover what I have known since youth. There is a physiological root in this response to expanding day length. With our common sedentary indoor mode of winter living comes the danger of light-induced depression of spirits. It might be more accurate to say that the reaction is induced by deprivation of light. My life has been too much involved with being out-of-doors in every season for me to be subject to that reaction to light; still, I believe it to be one of the most elemental of all biologic responses. I think of it as a pituitary reaction to the lengthening of day that follows the winter solstice, for that is the very moment of beginning of that great biologic-psychologic phenomenon that we in temperate climes call spring. With varying lag times involved, I believe, every vertebrate begins to prepare for spring in the winter solstice. Invertebrates, and perhaps plants too, might be found to follow a similar course, but I am not so sure of the sequence there.

First aired on WRVO-FM, Jan. 5, 1990.

What is the evidence of what I say? Well, the best way to respond to the seemingly unanswerable question may be a series of questions. What makes the horned owls begin their courtship right around Christmas? Why is the male fox on the move in January? Why do the normally innocuous skunks become so noxious as the New Year progresses toward spring? Why would the woodchuck make the seemingly inane blunder of venturing forth from a fairly secure den on February 2 into the depth of winter? Why would the maple sap begin to flow during a period of freeze and thaw? I know you don't have the answers to these questions, but can you see the pattern that hints at the answer?

Each of the creatures mentioned has a distinct lead time required in order for them to be ready for their moment in reproductive history. The male red fox has to locate a mate and consummate that process before the end of February if young are to be born in April. Gestation for the fox is fifty-one days. The skunk, too, is working on a similar deadline. With skunk, it is sixty-three days between mating and the birth of the young in May. Woodchuck mating cannot be far behind fox and skunk, since the young are born in April after a thirty-one day gestation. Horned owls, which seem more deliberate than these others, are shooting for nesting in February or early March since the incubation period is just over one month and there is a window of vulnerability during April and May for adult prey species, followed by the great increase in the birth of mice, rats, and rabbits.

The world of nature is a cyclic energy system, and the energy explosion that we call spring is not a spontaneous happenstance. Rather, it is a culminating phenomenon, and the latent energy that drives its beginnings is really an inheritance from the previous growing season. As soon as the days begin to lengthen, just before Christmas, internal changes triggered by lengthening daylight begin to prepare animals for the annual cycle of reproduction. This has to be timed so the growing appetite of new life will mesh with the expanding supply of food. No computer save nature's own could properly organize the complex energy patterns that match the growing appetite of the animal world with the developing supply of food and cover in plants.

Think of it. If rabbits, field mice, songbirds, and waterfowl were to miscalculate and erupt too early, the result could be disastrous. Occasionally we see that happen because weather, even though it is a facet of this great energy complex, is often unpunctual. It zigs when everything else is calling for a zag, momentarily freezing the course of spring's advance. In the main, however, this great complex of glandular reaction and hormonal flow, with its varied behavioral responses, is like an exquisitely adjusted machine. That is why my inner psyche, which usually doesn't even seem to be paying attention, exhibits the January-spring response every year right about this time.

What the Groundhog Told Me

There was a time when Groundhog Day was a simple celebration that people observed lightheartedly, if at all. Some people believed in it mildly. Others put it in roughly the same category as Santa Claus or the Tooth Fairy, either one of which, they knew, needs a lot of outside help to work their magic.

But now the groundhog has gone big time, even acquiring a stage name, Punxsutawney Phil, and enough hype and press agentry to earn a spot in most media newscasts, including a front-page feature in our local metropolitan newspaper. I hope Phil doesn't suffer under any delusions about his true role in the whole thing. Now that he's acquired a press agent and a stage name, he's become a symbol, a pawn of commercialism.

And I hope the Punxsutawney press agentry doesn't really believe that Phil's object in sallying forth from his sleeping chamber has anything to do with weather forecasting. It's biology, you know. True, he hasn't eaten for months, but on February 2 a groundhog can't do much about that. What really matters is that he hasn't seen a girl woodchuck in months, and he has a date with groundhog destiny. The survival of his kind is at stake.

Now, understand, I don't begrudge the Punxsutawnians their day in the national limelight, but I do feel a little concern about the effect on woodchuckdom of introducing show biz into their bucolic world. It goes something like this:

Originally published in the *Baldwinsville Messenger*, Feb. 8, 1978; first aired on WRVO-FM, Jan. 30, 1987.

What the Groundhog Told Me

Now the groundhog has gone big time, even acquiring a stage name, Punxsutawney Phil.

The scene is a Pennsylvania hillside. A huge crowd, including the national press, has crowded around a woodchuck hill. A bit tardily a furry head emerges from the hole. A cheer goes up from the crowd. "Phil!" "Phil!"

Phil blinks. "Boy, that sure is a bright sun! What's everybody doing out here anyway? You seen any girl woodchucks around?"

"Phil, would you step out into the sunlight, here, and tell us whether you see your shadow?"

"What for? Say you don't happen to have any alfalfa sprouts handy, do you? Well! No matter! I can wait for that. Haven't any of you fellows seen a girl around?"

"Listen, Phil, the whole nation's waiting to hear what you have to say about the arrival of spring."

"I'd say it's much too cold and snowy for spring yet. Now, about those girls."

"Phil, the national television cameras are trained on you. Will you get out here and do your thing!"

"No kidding. Where? Which one's on?"

"They're all on. Will you speak up and tell people when spring's going to arrive!"

"Okay, but what do I say? I don't know anything about weather forecasting. Why don't they ask a meteorologist?"

"Do you see your shadow there? That's supposed to mean there'll be six more weeks of winter."

"That's a laugh. I'll bet there'll be eight more weeks of winter whether the sun shines or not today. But I get the idea. Where do you want me to stand?"

"Over there! And would you try to smile a little!"

"Folks, I have an announcement to make. I have seen my shadow, so there will be six more weeks of winter. Can you buy that?"

General cheers. A few groans. Several people leaning in and waving at the cameras. Then a voice from the crowd!

"Say, Phil, someone just saw a pretty girl woodchuck over by the big oak tree."

"No kidding! Well, my manager says my schedule's pretty full today. A crew from Channel 8 is coming out for an in-depth interview this afternoon. I might be able to work her into my schedule sometime tomorrow or the next day. She's not available? Oh well, that's show biz!"

"Say, would you get somebody to drop in to a delicatessen and grab some greens! I'm famished."

Sic gloria transit Woodchuckdom.

The foregoing, of course, is really just a lighthearted commentary. The groundhog is not seriously threatened by this minor misinterpretation of the facts of life. Groundhog Day has been with us for ages, and during all those years groundhog populations have experienced a healthy prosperity. Still, there is such a thing as truth in packaging and I happen to be one who would rather see us spread truth about nature than fiction. So I wish the Punxsutawnians would get their facts straight and treat this whole event as the great romantic interlude that it really is and leave the predicting of spring to the robin or the Canada goose or the spring peepers. These guys usually have firsthand information and they don't go right back to bed as soon as the cameras leave.

Conserving

Trees laden with heaven's tears
stand green against the browning earth
   Once again an attempt
   has been made
To wash the universe of accumulating filth
Ah, but to no avail,
   Man simply dons his raincoat. —JWD

We suffer in America from a set of common conceits that do little to enhance our future prospects. One is that a warranty deed is a sole ownership allowing us to do with the land whatever we please. Some of us see this as a constitutional right, and we regard zoning, environmental impact requirements, and cost-benefit analysis, not to mention eminent domain, as some sort of purposeless socialist agenda designed to swell the ranks of government. Unfortunately, government has sometimes seemed to be confirming this point of view without adequately explaining its purpose.

Another common conceit, that water cycles, bioenergetics, and other living community dynamics are private property, have led to controversy. In reality, because all forces in nature are interrelated, they are public properties, a legacy from the past and an obligation to future generations. Some of the factors are clearly global in extent.

We tend to forget that our relationship with the environment is not simply an exercise of the senses. The air we breath, the water we drink, and the food we eat are all products of the environment. Only if we keep the environment healthy can we count on this life-support system.

In this section are presented essays that attempt to redefine our conceits and, without political angst, offer viewpoints and analyses that will help in the formation of informed opinion. The attempt is to enable us all to be good citizens of our community, promoting economic health without compromising the health of the environment.

On Appreciating Death

Many of these essays have been devoted to the energy and the beauty of the living world. You can understand that. It is this combination of beauty and powerful interaction that sustains our interest, making of us both naturalists and nature enthusiasts. Still, we can't study it long before we begin to appreciate the importance of that part of nature's machinery that we call death.

People who dwell on death are considered a bit strange, but I would submit that the naturalist is dealing with an entirely different aspect of death than is the necrophile. We are not concerned with souls or spirits here, but with the processes by which the myriad exquisite fabrications of nature, once dead, are removed from the landscape and reduced to an elemental state.

Take a woodlot well populated with trees, shrubs, and herbs and vibrant with the songs, calls, and movements of the creatures that inhabit them. Concentrate for just a moment on what happens beyond this compelling facade. On any given day, hundreds of pounds of tree and shrub branches and foliage may crash to the ground. Dozens of the creatures meet up with some cruel fate that reduces them to inert remains of once vibrant life. In time such remnants would begin to pile up and impede the life processes, even choke off the regeneration of new life, were it not for the dark system we are here discussing. Without this process of death and decay, life itself would be threatened. If we could sweep an area clear of all dead life, go back to square one, we could observe that.

What we do observe is an ongoing process into which each new

First aired on WRVO-FM, Nov. 12, 1993.

166 | Conserving

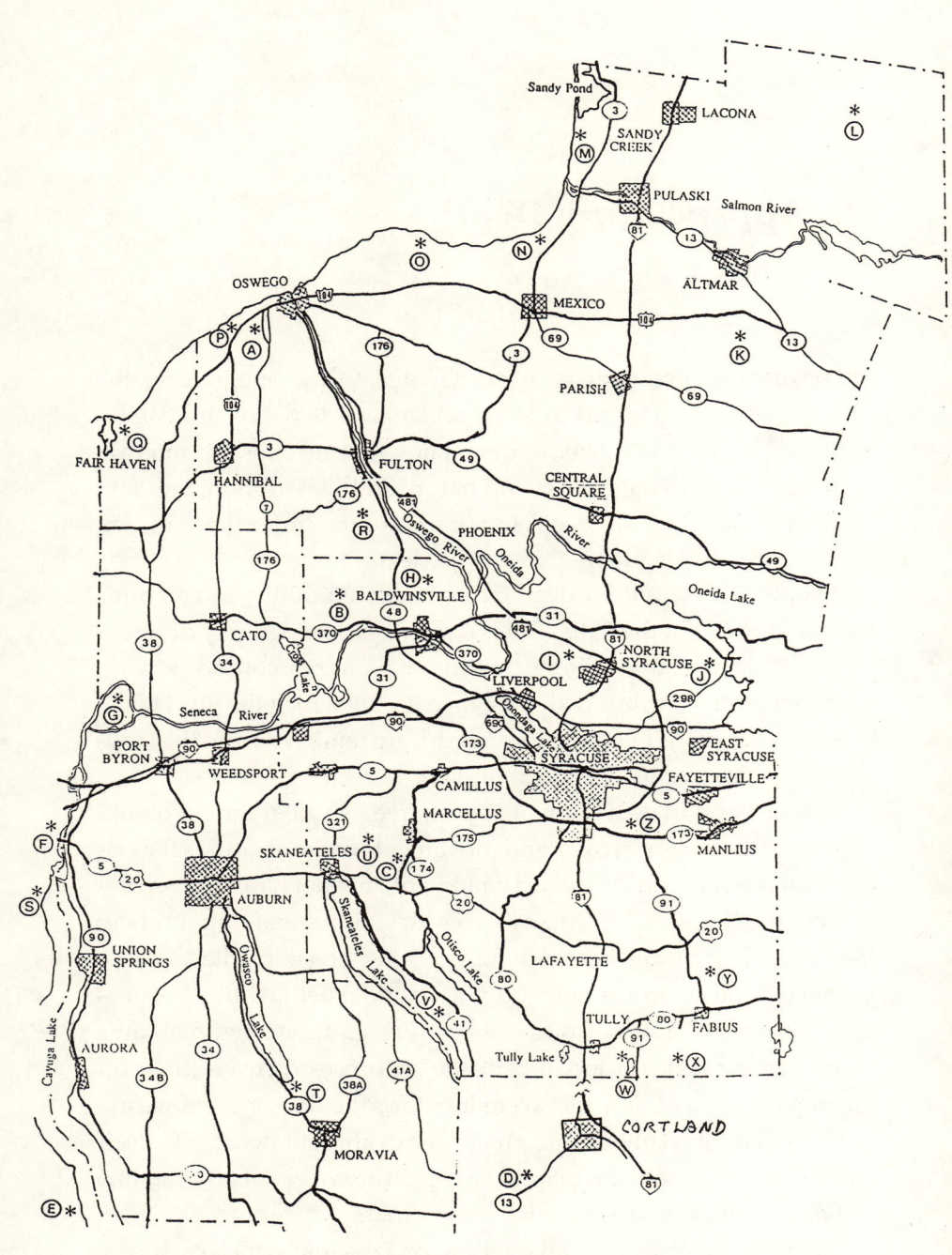

Central New York nature areas (key at right).

terminated life-form settles without a hitch. The process has two cycles. One is initiated by the vulture, the fox, or the crow, those creatures that don't demand living protein. The second cycle is the similar activities of insects and other creatures that find dead plant life to their liking. These activities are the visible phases of the dismemberment of former life. Unseen but often more pivotal is the work of many minute plant and animal-like creatures, the bulk of them microscopic: bacteria, protozoa, fungi, and the like. The process they initiate is not dismemberment and removal. It is more one of defabrication, with the gradual return of all those remnants of earlier energy cycles to a state where they are ready to initiate new episodes of synthesis.

We can tag these varied agents of breakdown with the more specific monikers *scavengers, transformers,* and *decomposers.* Their role is to reverse what the processes of photosynthesis, assimilation, and growth have produced to prepare them to initiate a new cycle of life.

A. Rice Creek Field Station
B. Beaver Lake Nature Center
C. Baltimore Woods Nature Center
D. Lime Hollow Nature Center
E. Cayuga Nature Center
F. Montezuma National Wildlife Refuge
G. Howland Island
H. Three Rivers
I. Clay Marsh
J. Cicero Swamp
K. Happy Valley
L. Little John
M. Eldorado Shores
N. Derby Hill
O. Noyes Sanctuary
P. Snake Swamp
Q. Fair Haven Bay
R. Ox Creek
S. Cayuga Lake Shoreline
T. Owasco Flats
U. Gully Road Pond
V. Skaneateles Lake
W. Labrador Pond
X. Shackham Road Forest
Y. Old Fly Natural Area
Z. Clark Reservation
*WMA = Wildlife Management Area

Thus tissues become amino acids and finally carbon dioxide, water, nitrates, phosphates, and the other elements of life: the ashes to ashes and dust to dust scenario known to the ancients of biblical times.

This is the primary strategy of the natural system, the only assurance of immortality that exists in nature, the assurance that all existing life will in time give substance to new life. All of this dissection of the once living that follows death points out a flaw in our value judgments about our secret benefactors, the agents of decomposition.

I had a homely example of this a few years back when riding to a conference with a young biologist, schooled in the traditions of those times, a cellular biologist. It was that time of the year following the reproductive season when the number of road kills had dramatically increased. At first he railed a bit about the fact that we had no system for removing these carcasses from the road. We went on until he spotted a freshly killed rabbit on which several crows had descended. "Those rascals," my young colleague expounded, "they're clever. No matter how hard you try, you can't ever hit the black devils."

I am sure my mouth dropped open, but he probably didn't notice. Questioning turned up the fact that he didn't hold very high opinions of any predators, hawk, owl, or fox, and he had an even lower opinion of vultures and others that would feed on dead meat.

His attitude toward bacteria and fungi, on the other hand, was quite enlightened. He acknowledged that there certainly were beneficial bacteria and that mushrooms and other decomposer organisms were vital to the process of preparing the products of death and of excretion to become the raw materials for the development of new life.

At this point, I asked him if he didn't think it inconsistent to criticize anonymous folks for not removing road kills and at the same time make a game of trying to hit crows that were engaged in removing them in a natural way. He didn't. "You can't hit 'em anyway and I still don't like the idea of leaving the whole thing up to those rascals."

Well, I let it go at that, but an important point had been made for me. The authors of decomposition need a press agent because their role is important to us but our level of appreciation is mighty low.

Recycling and the Honey Wagon

Recycling has become a household word. People are increasingly knowledgeable about it as a potential relief for the growing solid-waste dilemma. Still, many have, at best, a primitive understanding of its nature-related history. Most believe it to be a new concept drawn up by local governments harassed by the problems of growing waste and shrinking landfill potential. I entertained this and similar thoughts as I witnessed an age-old example of recycling, well-known to bird-watchers and other nature enthusiasts.

Often in the middle of winter, the dairy farmer finds it necessary to reduce the growing mountain of waste product from the cow barn. He loads it on a manure spreader. Many call that churning, spewing machine a honey wagon in complete contradiction of fact and obfuscation of process. The honey wagons have been busy this week, covering the fields with their fragrant product, not quite honey but certainly not caca to an old farm boy, and an event of some poesy to a naturalist.

It's a simple concept. Let's review it, starting with the cow. Cows have a simple lifestyle, right? They eat, sleep, give milk or their all to their master herdsman. It's the ultimate in sacrificial living. Not really simple, however, because the cow's choice of food, grass, hay and fodder, and lots of liquid really complicates its life. That stuff is so hard to digest. It is a full-time job for the cow, which can't just swallow and forget about it. It must mix it internally, regurgitate it, re-chew it, and subject it to bacterial and protozoal action before it can begin to get any nourishment from what it swallows.

First aired on WRVO-FM, Jan. 25, 1991.

Anyone who watches a cow for any length of time is aware that it is an amazing but not very efficient biological machine. A high percentage of what it ingests goes right straight through its four so-called stomachs and its elaborate intestinal system without giving much nourishment. Cow watchers also learn how much water the process requires.

Those who study what emerges from the cow (there are those who do, you know) might fault me here for missing the forest for the trees. Still I've made a start. After all, the subject here is recycling.

This growing pile of noxious stuff, to which the cow adds daily—really hourly—has to be disposed of. If the dairyman were a householder, he'd put it all in plastic garbage bags and set it out at the curb. It's a ridiculous thought, I know, but it makes its point, reminding us of something. If the cow is truly biologically inefficient, the householder is absolutely impossible, completely off the scale of ecological efficiency. After all, the cow's waste will have completely disappeared by midsummer. The householder who wished to look for it could find that pile of varied wastes twenty years later, much of it unchanged.

You can accuse me here of comparing apples and peaches. After all, our biological wastes are neatly disposed of. To the world we live in, however, it doesn't matter whether it's apples or peaches. It all has to be dealt with. We can't ignore the peach pits if we really want to understand recycling.

Anyway, let's get back to the honey wagon, which, for all its bad odor, is a lot more sanitary than the garbage truck. The manure spreader is a recycling agent, as is the cow. The spreader takes what the cow can't handle and returns it to the land. The garbage truck takes what we can't handle and places it in a hermetically sealed vault. It would be entirely inappropriate to suggest that the garbage truck then returns our wasteful by-products to their source.

The manure, when spread on the snow or on the bare soil, is an object of interest to varieties of wild things, large and small. In summer we note beetles and flies. In winter we find birds: horned larks, buntings, crows, starlings, and rockdoves, to name a few. They congregate on the freshly spread manure in search of undigested seeds or other edibles.

You may shudder at the thought, but that's recycling. What remains after all the gleaning we can observe is a great deal of gleaning we can't observe, performed by creatures too small for the naked eye. Bacteria and fungi also get into the act. The upshot of all of these varied activities is a defabrication of all this waste from complex carbohydrates, proteins, and fats to simpler things such as basic compounds of carbon, hydrogen, oxygen, nitrogen, phosphorous, and sulfur. In this form they can be used to manufacture a new generation of complex carbohydrates, proteins, and fats.

Do you begin to get the idea of recycling in nature? New generations of life are fed by new generations of foodstuffs that are the legacy from past generations of life and foodstuffs.

Compare the genius of that system with the poverty of the roadside system we employ, and remember that the only part of that mess that has a remote chance of feeding a future generation is what you put in the recycling bin, if you live in a county with recycling. We've got to do better than that.

The Changing Seasons

This is a pivotal moment in the sweep of the seasons when the display of the woodland flowers begins to wane and the calico fields have little more than scattered patches of golden dandelion to recommend them to our view. In our yards, tulips and lilacs are approaching their full glory and the fresh-mowed lawns are at their brightest with here and there a blotch or a streak of pale blue veronica to break the green monotony.

The abandoned pastures, now crowded with shrubs and small trees (cornel, shad, apple, and wild cherry) are lightly dusted with white or pale pink. Beneath the tender green veil of burgeoning leaves, robin, song sparrow, and house finch are incubating fragile spheres of life. A shallow depression in a weed field harbors a half dozen baby cottontails huddled together in anticipation of just a few more days of mother's milk before they must desert their downy bower and launch forth on their own, facing all the hazards that implies. Their success is in their sheer numbers. Individually, theirs is a chancy lot.

Just inside the edge of the woodlot, a young doe has deposited her first fawn, whose prospects for survival are much better than those of any single cottontail. Here numbers, meaning overpopulation, may actually be the greatest threat to reaching adulthood. The time of highest hazard for the fawn may be its first winter when the older, taller deer divest the coverts of all edible food to a point above its reach.

First aired on WRVO-FM, May 11, 1990.

Taller deer divest the coverts of all edible food.

But fawns and baby cottontails are not the staple for the average roadside viewer in early May. This is the time to ply the fields and hedgerows for that annual burst of feathered blossoms, the high tide of songbird migration. As long as I can remember, I have cherished those May mornings when grosbeaks, tanagers, and warblers proclaim their colorful presence from the blossoming apple or the emerging beech. This performance has always seemed to me an outdoor operetta full of song and color and meaningful movement. It is a sad coincidence, however, that as its audience grows—today there are more nature enthusiasts than ever—the frequency and variety of the performance dwindles.

It is particularly disturbing that one of the few events in nature that can pry us from our television sets and bring us out to view the natural world that supports us may soon reach the point when the only place we can see it in all its glory may be through archive tapes broadcast on television. Here, it will be sandwiched in between sporting events, forgettable distortions of the human condition, or ads for hair replacements or depilatories. That's a depressing scenario, hardly in the mainstream of the public interest. Still I can't escape a bit of wonderment that people who will band together to fight over landfills to assure that their local garbage will be deposited in someone else's neighborhood but will not send a concerted message to the seats of government to protest the violence we are doing to the planet.

I realize that the local threat is very real to people. I agree with them about the undesirability of a landfill in my backyard, but I realize too that I may not forever expect to be privileged to export my garbage elsewhere. Having grown up in a rural setting, I could actually wish for a neighbor who would reintroduce the chanticleer to my sunrise ritual. However, out of consideration for my good neighbors who have different backgrounds than my own, I wouldn't presume to bring chickens, goats, or rabbits to this staid suburban setting. I agree that they belong in the country.

When we consider the ritual of bird migration, however, we are examining a bellwether of environmental health. We can ill afford to reach the point where, as Leopold has put it in memorializing the fate of the passenger pigeon, "Men still live who remember pigeons. Trees still live who, in their youth, were shaken by a living wind. But a decade hence only the oldest oaks will remember, and at long last only the hills will know."

Lamenting changes in lifestyles is an exercise for the silver-haired, but concern about the health of the planet should be every citizen's responsibility. However you come down on this particular issue, I urge you to get out into the back roads or even to the woodsides this week to welcome the returning feathered hoards. It may be that some day people's passion for a changing world will cancel the performance, and soon neither the patriarch oaks nor the living hills themselves will remember the warblers.

CO_2 and the Next Ice Age

A recent item on National Public Radio provided insight on a matter that has been of interest to me for some time. The item dealt with some studies done abroad that attempted to explain glacial ages through the analysis of Ice Age atmosphere trapped in the ancient ice packs of some of the world's great glaciers. The most significant finding appears to have been that this Ice Age air, for whatever reason, is significantly deficient in carbon dioxide.

If you wonder how that possibly could be the cause, or perhaps be symptomatic of the glacier, think of our present concerns about the greenhouse effect when burning fossil fuels adds carbon dioxide to the atmosphere. Carbon dioxide in the atmosphere works like an insulator or a heat trap. Deficient carbon dioxide would allow excessive heat loss. If lower carbon dioxide levels were, indeed, a cause and not just a symptom, we should be able to trace some chain of events that led to it.

Let's examine the present sources and reservoir of carbon dioxide. It is said that 50 percent of our earth-entrained carbon dioxide supply is in the oceans. With present climate, a good portion of that ocean mass is relatively warm at the surface, even though it hovers around 40° Fahrenheit in the depths. Similarly, the major consumers of carbon dioxide would appear to be the vast underwater forests of marine plants and the even greater concentrations of photosynthetic plankton organisms. Remember, carbon dioxide is consumed and oxygen released in the process of photosynthesis.

First aired on WRVO-FM, Nov. 25, 1988.

Okay! you may be thinking. Wouldn't cooling of the ocean inhibit all that? Yes and no. The capacity of liquids to absorb gases decreases as the temperature rises, increases as it falls. In addition, we find some of our greatest concentrations of plankton in the polar oceans. So cooling doesn't necessarily result in decreased CO_2 consumption by the oceans. Somehow marine plants are able to accomplish what terrestrial plants cannot.

None of this, however, explains why the cooling occurs in the first place. Up to now, assumptions have centered on erratic solar radiation and the eccentric orbit of the earth, but it's pretty difficult to say how and why those grand cycles of cooling appear. If carbon dioxide reduction is at the heart of the phenomenon, how do we bring that about? The suggestion that cooler oceans might have increased absorption capacity appears to be only part of the answer.

Let's look at the sources of carbon dioxide production, too. Burning of organic compounds is the basis. Put a log on the fire, start the car, turn on the furnace and you've set into motion oxygen-consuming, carbon-dioxide-producing reactions, both inside and outside the body. Breathe in the good air, breathe out the bad air. Oxygen = good, CO_2 = bad.

Remember, too, that even green plants, which are our principal sources of net oxygen production during the day, consume oxygen and produce carbon dioxide at night. Even the process of decay is an oxygen-consuming process, and one of the products overlooked because of all the smelly by-products is CO_2. What this all says is that one way to cut down on carbon dioxide production would be to reduce terrestrial animal life and cut down on decay.

Now, if you are still with me, you are aware that we have talked about some important mechanisms for CO_2 reduction, but we've not established at all whether they are causative factors or reaction to cooling. In the final analysis, both energy budgets and energy distribution are at the heart of things.

When we talk about energy distribution, we are talking about weather and ocean movement and here is where these most recent studies have laid a portion of the blame. Changes in ocean currents are the mightiest earthbound causative factors. Think of El Nino and worldwide droughts.

But then, how do we explain the changes in ocean current that might be the causative factors? I'm not sure I know the answer, but I'm not at a loss for words. I've been saying for years that our great global ecosystems are like great interacting machines. If you tinker with the elements, you may very well drastically alter the results.

At present, we are consumed with the specter of advancing worldwide deserts, melting ice caps, rising oceans that consume real estate: all the result of our present carbon dioxide production. If you look behind the scenery, you may have pause to think. The net product of all this greenhouse stuff is sure to be lowered CO_2 production and net gain CO_2 consumption by the oceans as temperatures lower. Remember, it only takes a few degrees' shift from our present norm to take us in either direction.

What am I trying to say? Wake up!! The real danger to the future of life as we know it is not just in the Kremlin or in the Middle East, and nuclear deterrents are hardly promising when we're talking about CO_2. We need to preserve the steady state.

Environmental sanity is not optional, depending on budget and economy. Such thinking is bush league. The rules of conservation of nature and conservation of energy are laws, not recommendations.

Creating an Environmental Bill of Rights

Here we are a week and a half into the new year and I find myself automatically falling into a speculative mood. It's natural, isn't it? By now, each of us has applied some measure of evaluation to the events of the past year and wondered a bit about the future.

I've looked at the past year and I see a few trends of interest. The environment made a few gains, even scored a few real victories, but on balance there was a net loss, which means that we and our children's children are somewhat the poorer for last year.

I would rate the following as worthy of note. At least someone talked about the massive inconsistency in the government's promoting the misuse of federal forests, rangeland, and mineral resources. They talked about it, but all that showed us was that no one is sure who is really in charge. The news media always play with the human political struggles and don't really define the environmental reasons for ending these raids on our federally owned resources. My score for this one: powerful special interests, ten; future environmental health, three. No real change there.

Then there is the destruction of tropical rainforests, the disappearance of neotropical songbirds, and the extinction of potentially vital plant and animal species. This was a major subject in environmental journals, but, again, there was a confused picture from the media.

Published as "Counting 1994's Net Loss for Environment," in the *Herald-Journal,* Jan. 10, 1995 (The Herald Co., Syracuse, NY © Herald-Journal/The Post-Standard. All rights reserved. Reprinted with permission).

The most oft-quoted line I heard this year was, "Well, we can't tell those people how to use their resources." It's a puny thought that ignores how much we are already involved in the pressures that motivate the squandering of an irretrievable resource. The transformation of rainforest to pasture is a strategical nightmare, a short-term financial gain for what could be a permanent costly loss.

Despite their limited extent, rainforests have an inordinate effect on global conditions. My score here: myopic entrepreneurship, 250; rainforests, one. That's the ratio of living environment lost per acre when we remove trees and insert cows.

Well, you get the idea, and I know that if I continue in this vein a moment longer, even my environmental readers will desert me. The point here is that while the American dream is based on a maximum of freedom to follow our own desires, especially on our own land, there is a need for caution and even at times restraint. When it comes to our natural assets, we need to recognize the difference between use and destruction.

The last election provided us with some good young legislators determined to see our government return to its traditional form and function. My caution to them as they address themselves to this feat of political and fiscal prestidigitation: consider these ten environmental commandments ordained of old by someone far above us.

1. The sun is the source. You shall adopt no earthly barrier to its provision of healthful full-spectrum energy.

2. You shall create no icon or idol, be it jobs, wealth, or lifestyle that destroys the health of an ecosystem.

3. Take not the name of the environment in vain, using meaningless synonyms for *provident,* such as "liberal," "fuzzy-headed," or "idealistic."

4. All ecosystems need both rest and respect appropriate to their worth. Recognize an environmental sabbath for ailing ecosystems.

5. Honor the soil, water, and atmosphere as well as the role of green plants. They are the parents of all life, even yours.

6. Do not destroy species without remorse or concern for the consequences.

7. Make no international alliances that demean the capacity of the planet to support life.

8. Do not squander nonrenewable resources when alternative renewable sources can be developed.

9. Cease the use of statistics that ignore long-term effects on the planet's life-support systems.

10. Do not covet another nation's resources without paying both the full value and the environmental IOUs that harvest methods predict.

I haven't mentioned God in all this, but I would suggest that the creator is watching. Is anyone down here listening?

A Message from a Pretty Gifted Grosbeak

This is not what I'd call the thinking man's era either in politics or in life. I grant you, that's the environmentalist's view of politics. Only a few of my closest friends see it the way I do. That's probably good. I learn a lot from people who disagree with me.

My father, who I've always considered to be a thinking man, warned me that there aren't many people who give priority to long-term views. It's hard enough, they say, to deal with things here and now. Conservation is a luxury that deprives us of too much of our present needs.

In case you haven't guessed, I've got a peculiar problem that's troubling me right now. I have four precious grandchildren, the total output from five semiprecious children. (Sorry, kids, but you're on your own right now and a part of the decision-making process that's not really dealing with what I want to talk about.)

Anyway, I have these four grandchildren and I am trying to write them into my will without either money or other substantial worldly goods to incorporate. I can pass along a philosophy of life that suggests that some self-denial now will provide heightened future benefits. I can also pass along a kind of schizophrenic combination of joy at being alive and fascination at finding out how things work, or don't work, without taking them on as causes.

But those are actually things I am simply passing along from their

First aired on WRVO-FM, Sept. 30, 1994.

grandparents. In philosophy, I am a true hybrid of my mother's and father's priorities. It's when I get down to thinking about my own unique contributions that I run into trouble.

From one standpoint, the children might find a glimmer of success in my life. I've had four different careers, and there is some lasting fallout on the landscape from each one. That's my pride talking. Not much in that for them. From another standpoint, however, I've been a dismal failure. The great surpassing moments in my life, the things that have made the most lasting impression on me, outside of my family, seem unlikely to survive me.

Let me list a few of those moments:

The time in my life, while still an elementary student, when I first witnessed the spring explosion of northward-moving warblers. It was as if someone had just released a carload of butterflies. I sat in the crotch of an English walnut looking across my neighbor's garden at their blossoming cherries. I put significant wear on my *Reed's Bird Guide* that day and added ten species to my mythical life list. It's mythical because I don't actually keep a list.

The sound and color of that treasured moment defy description. That moment had many clones in my youth. Can I take my grandchildren someplace today and bestow that priceless treasure on them? Not a chance. They'll have to read about it.

How about the annual joy of the first oriole, or tanager, or rose-breasted grosbeak singing from the summit of a partly leafed-out beech or maple? I can share that experience if I hurry, but the prognosis for the future of those birds is distinctly similar to the warbler scenario.

What about the enchanting complexity of a northern wetland community, alive with life above, beneath, and at the surface of the water. Not too rich a prospect there, either. Most of the best ones I knew thirty years ago have been drained or have otherwise suffered a major breakdown in their machinery.

I'd like to convey to those grandchildren some essence of the exciting moment when I first realized how truly complex and utterly fascinating and important, beyond the ken of all but the Godhead, was a single acre of rainforest. By the time the kids get to care about that, most of the acreage may have changed from five million cubic feet of bustling intermeshing forest life to eleven thousand cubic feet of grass, peopled and slowly being overwhelmed by a few hundred pounds of red meat on the hoof.

I'm not just ranting here. There is real substance in these examples of lost opportunities. You can't eat them, but they do have a potent message. We adults are not doing too well right now. Our priorities are not concerned with what things will be like when you children are adults. I say, put us all out to graze in those dull tropical pastures that once were vibrant rainforests and force us to listen to the gentle warbling of the grosbeaks.

I'll translate the grosbeak's message for you. "It's the environment, not politics, that will feed you tomorrow. That nourishing environment is your hope for the future. What will this world be like when you're trying to catalogue your legacy for your grandchildren? With species growing extinct everyday, it looks to me like I won't even be there to advise you."

Pretty gifted grosbeak. Too bad we can't train grosbeaks to form political think tanks. Sometimes a new perspective really helps.

Spotted Owl

Issue or Icon?

I had a chance to travel to Utica College recently to deliver a talk to a group of biologists. My subject was the role of biologists in providing perspective to a public required to make value judgments on issues for which it is often poorly informed, even in the midst of plentiful media coverage.

I enjoyed the trip. They're nice people at Utica College. Afterward we had a chance to discuss the issues, and one thing that came up was the difference between soft news coverage and headline or hard news coverage. Features may often provide excellent background, but the hard news to which most people pay attention often gets focused on side issues.

Take the logging of federal rain forests in the northwest. The issue is the preservation of the spotted owl against the maintenance of jobs, right? Isn't that what almost everyone thinks? But let's look a little deeper. With all the primeval forest in private hands forty years ago, why is it necessary today for private loggers to make their living on federal land? Have they systematically ravaged their private holdings? Or have the number of people trying to make a living in forestry increased beyond the capacity of the forest land to support them?

One fact that any biologist could certify: the coastal ranges were once covered with magnificent, lush rain forest. Most of the mature

First aired on WRVO-FM, Nov. 23, 1990.

forest is now gone from private land. Under systematic logging, the mature old-growth forest on public land is shrinking, too. Small wonder that those who understand the values of untouched forest, both present and future, are alarmed by these trends. After all, something of value to them is threatened. They have no real rights or leverage on what the logging industry does on private land, but they do feel that they have the right, if not the duty, to raise the questions they do about the same practices on federal land. Use of that land impinges on all of us. That's the first issue of relevance.

What is the owl? The owl is an icon, a religious symbol. Beyond that it is also an instrument of convenience. There is no other clear issue upon which those who practice abuse on federal land can be brought to task. We do have an endangered species act. We don't have an endangered habitats act. For those whose religion holds that unfettered nature is the ultimate good, the spotted owl has become the lever.

However, there is an issue that hasn't been addressed. Saving wilderness might not save the spotted owl. If the spotted owl should disappear, would the reason for limiting logging have evaporated? And how about the issue of jobs? It may seem inhumane to suggest that jobs, too, are an icon, a symbol in a different religion that holds that a man has a right to a job he chooses. I think if I were a logger working in those great northwest forests I'd be an adherent to that religion. You probably would, too.

How, then, can jobs be an icon? First we have to look at the nature of the jobs. Logging is a profession whose practice can result in the destruction of the factory that supports it. That's not the purpose of the logger, but on private land out there, the evidence that the factory is being degraded is strong. And the common good is now perceived to be the systematic harvest of publicly owned resources. No one should be amazed that there are people who do not want to see public forests devastated the way many private forests have been.

At the same time, we shouldn't make the assumption that these northwest loggers are a bunch of despoilers, so sanguine for forest products that they'd cut anything. They point with pride to their record of reforestation. They also talk a good conservation game, but their ecological message is suspect, badly skewed by some value judgments about what is bad and good in nature. Some of these judgments have no validity except to those trying to preserve jobs.

So in this way the two religions confront each other, and the zealots on each side talk no compromise. And that's the way it is reported in the news. Owls and jobs, the icons, not the basic principles.

The only thing that matters is this. Despite the reforestation and a few other conservation practices, are the jobs wiping out the factory? Does the harvest exceed the replacement? I've never even heard that issue addressed in the broad national coverage of the issue. I've seen hundreds of shots of spotted owls and loggers standing beside young reforestation plots and dozens of interviews with families frightened by the prospect of job loss, but not one chart or graph analyzing the effect of all this logging on the standing reserve or of the effect of clear-cutting on forest reestablishment. If the harvest rate is exceeding the reproductive capacity of the resource, and the evidence seems to indicate that it is, then the jobs that exist are only temporary at best.

A really public-spirited legislator or executive should look past the icons and see the issues. People still have the right to despoil their own land, but public land is another matter. If we protect our public land properly, the spotted owl, the soil base, and at least limited forestry will survive.

In the process, of course, a good many loggers and forest products people may have to find new professions. But that's the nature of things. Do we stop it now while we still have the resource, or do we wait until the jobs are gone because the harvestable resource is gone?

The Last Setting of the Table

One of the charms of fall, for me at least, rests in its eternal changeability. It isn't simply a matter of changing colors or falling leaves, nor is it just the frosty nights, which put us in mind of rustling cornstalks and golden pumpkins.

There are spirits riding the night winds that have never seen the witch's broom or heard the goblin's wild call. They are the omens of approaching winter, the ghosts of a contracting world, which hurl a warning to some and a challenge to others. They seem to say, "This is the last setting of the table 'til spring rolls in again. Prepare yourself to live on that which you see before you, or begone." Robin, wren, and wild goose do depart, while grouse and rabbit prepare for a change of menu.

This is an age-old cry, and yet, it wasn't always thus. The time was when this area basked in the warmth of a tropic sun. Lush green vegetation persisted throughout the year. This era has left its stamp upon the land in the form of coal and oil deposits. Evidence of warmer times since the last glaciation is found in the pollen of southern trees in the peat deposits. In other eras, a thick mantle of heavy moving ice covered this same land. It ground and gouged the earth, leaving lakes and hills where none had ever been before. It also left square mile upon square mile of barren, almost sterile fields and great expanses of rock and gravel or sand upon which no tree or bird was found.

It is one of the great wonders of the natural community that it has

Published in the *Norwich Evening Sun*, Oct. 26, 1966; first aired on WRVO-FM, Dec. 1, 1989.

Robin, wren, and wild goose depart, while grouse and rabbit prepare for a change of menu.

the power to invade such forbidding areas and, starting simply with lichen and algae, to build an accumulating richness that one day can support a mighty forest. Today, tree-clothed hills and corn-clad valleys remain our endowment from ages past. Both plants and soil are cumulative products of time and evolution.

The animal community, too, has evolved through cycles of change that have seen strange fish, dinosaurs, flying reptiles, and huge land mammals appear, increase in numbers and then dwindle, some to disappear forever. The blood relationship of our present-day fauna to those titans of the past is involved and difficult to chart, but nevertheless very real. Even the precious supplies of fresh water that we tap from deep in the ground may be prehistoric in origin.

Viewed from a historic standpoint, all the wealth of the world that we enjoy may be the largess of past ages. In a very real sense this is true, yet the past has never seen anything like modern man. Judged beside the explosive growth of population and living standard, the forces of evolution and accumulation seem slow and inadequate. On balance, we seem to be approaching a resource autumn, and as I ponder this I hear echoes of the spirits' call, in voices far more ancient and timeworn, "This is the last setting of the table. Prepare yourself to live on that which you see before you or begone."

Do not be diverted by the thought that every year spring rolls in again, bringing with it renewal and new vitality, for every spring is different, and in terms that mean the most to us, infinitesimally poorer for the change. Think hard upon the implications of these progressions: primitive to civilized, rural to urban, sparsity to multitude, and you will see the urgency of understanding the work of ancient and modern forces.

Conservation education is not just for hunter, fisherman, and nature lover. We all have a stake in it, for we are all subject to and affected by the forces of change. Neither is conservation education an essential for the survival of man, at least not for the present. Certainly, however, since all wealth today, both intrinsic and temporal, is founded in our natural resources, conservation is a matter of concern for all.

Then there is the fact that wilderness, woodland, or marshland communities have not the same assurance of survival as has man. We already number the great northeastern forests primeval, the passenger pigeon, and the great auk as casualties in man's quest for survival. Around us we can still see such walking ghosts as the California condor, the blue whale, and the Everglades. One wonders how long they will survive.

When these things will pass, or why, is a matter of complete indifference to too many people, who never really lament anything until after it is gone and then blame conservationists for letting it go.

The greatest reason for conservation education today is this: we are today in our resource autumn, and we do have to plan to live on that which we see before us. If we do not plan wisely, though we may stay, the natural area will soon be gone.

Annual Four–Minute Environmental Teach–In

I know I'm a bit late, but I'd like to talk about New Year's resolutions. Before you tune out, I'd like to say, "Sure I know they don't work, but you'll have to admit the practice is a survivor. It's really not a bad idea for us to take a look at ourselves: to take stock and to try to change our courses."

You've already made your resolutions, if you still actually do such things, so I can't make any for you, but I would like to try a parallel course and offer to you John Weeks's Annual Four-Minute Environmental Teach-In.

Listening to National Public Radio's call-in program on the most important events of the year, I was pleased to see that a few people opted for environmental problems and was intrigued to see that something called "The Lie," meaning politically slanted information from Washington, tied for first place in importance. That's relevant! I've had a few things to say about misinformation on high myself during the last year.

So, let's define a couple of terms. One of the keynotes in the distorting of facts deals with the difference between an environmentalist and an ecologist. The former is an advocate, the latter is a student of the science of ecology. The ecologist may or may not be an activist but is the most likely of anyone to have the straight dope on the subject. My formal education is in plant and animal ecology. My experi-

First aired on WRVO-FM, Jan. 10, 1992.

ence is more in education than in practice of the science, but I believe I have a pretty good idea of what an ecologist would like me to say.

First. It's important for us to remember that stripped of our automobiles, flush toilets, refrigerators, and, yes, even our clothing, we are just bipedal mammals. "And pretty spectacular, at that," you may be thinking. Remarkable, indeed, but measured against the other creatures who variously inhabit our far-flung ranges, pretty puny.

That leads us to the second point. Technology allows us to fool ourselves as to the soundness of our relationships with our world. Most of us tend to believe we can continue to degrade the world and not suffer any consequence. Wrong. We're already suffering: financially, politically, physically, and spiritually. If you can accept that premise, you're ready to move on with me. If you can't accept it, you'd better get busy and study. It might save you all sorts of future distress. Might even save your life.

Let's look at survival for a minute. What are our basic needs for survival? Big bank account, fancy home, big car, power? Don't be silly. Most of the world's population has very little of that, and their chances of survival are sometimes as good as yours. Better in some cases.

What you really need is clean air to breathe, et cetera; pure water to support living, et cetera; good soil to nourish plant and animal life, et cetera; healthy plants to convert sun's energy to forms we can use, et cetera; and diverse animal life to distribute and equalize that useful energy, et cetera. So far no argument! Right?

The problem is all of those *et ceteras.* They include such obvious things as eating, drinking, keeping warm, keeping cool, having a roof over our head, and that's only the tip of the iceberg. It's those et ceteras, which most of us know too little about, that spell out the strategy of survival. Together they constitute the environmental law, a law that if I were a religious man, and I am, I would call God's law.

If you don't want to accept that classification, accept this: the law of the environment transcends and supersedes the laws, the cupidity, and the conceits of man. Just take a look at a few things: the ozone layer, air quality (what the air contains), water quality (what the water carries and deposits), plant distribution (with a heavy emphasis on our forests), and soil capacities (the ability of the soil to produce a harvestable nutritious food and fiber supply). All I'm going to say about those things is to urge you to study any of the following:

1. The effect of ozone layer loss on the safety of exposure to sunlight!

2. The effect of air pollution on the survival of people with respiratory limitations.

3. The effect of water quality on its ability to absorb carbon dioxide.

4. The effect of rainforest removal on climate control and on oxygen production and consumption.

5. The effect of the abuse of soils on the earth's productivity and its ability to cycle nutrients.

6. Et cetera.

The study might lead to a good if somewhat overwhelming New Year's resolution. Just try to get at one or two of them. After all, we've got maybe two decades before it will be too late to be as ignorant as we are today.

Well, that's all for this year. In next year's teach-in I hope to spend the whole four minutes talking about the environment.

Index

Achilles, Lillian, xviii
abscission layer, 117
Adirondack lake, 126
Aesop, 129
Agassiz, Louis, xvii
agriculture: colonial development of, 34–35; meadow, 84–85; air pressure and, 12
Albion, N.Y., 19–21
altricial nestling, 62
American Indians: war bonnet of, 129; traditions of, 155
amino acids, 168
amphibians, 65; bull frog, 54, 77; green frog, 54, 77; leopard frog, 43; spring peeper, 43, 52–54, 65; toad, 43, 52, 65; wood frog, 43, 52
anthocyanin, 118
Appalachian Highlands, 35
apples, 8
April, 43–45
Arabia, 11
Argentina, 84
assimilation, 167
atmosphere, 37
Audubon, John James, xvii, 19; paintings of, 128
automobiles: viewing of wildlife from, 67–69, early 20th century, 97
autumn: characteristics, 25–28, 104, 187; bird behavior, 110–12; and September, 107–9; and November's dialogue, 132–34

Baker Al (newspaper editor), xxi
Baltimore Woods: bobolink around, 85; August walk in, 99–101
barns, 13–15
Beard, Dan, 10
Beaver Lake Nature Center, xxi
Bergerson, Carl, xix
birds (alien species): albatross, 61; black cock, 29; capercaille, 29; European starling, 29; gray partridge, 24; house sparrow, 29–30, 91, 95; kiwi, 61; peacock, 129; red grouse, 29; ring-necked pheasant, 17, 24, 30–32, 62, 64, 100
birds (native species): blackbird family—Baltimore oriole, 8, 22, 61, 134, 272, bobolink, 5, 61, 108, 119–21, cowbird, 61, common grackle, 65, meadowlark, 65, red-winged blackbird, 91, 96, 121; bitterns and herons, 79; catbird, 8, 110; cedar waxwing, 110, 111; chickadee, 26–27; crows and jays, 25, 85, 93, 144; cuckoos, 8, 22; doves and pigeons—mourning dove, 22,

193

194 | Index

birds (native species) (*cont.*)
64, 144, passenger pigeon, 108, 120, 124; ducks, geese, and swans—ducks, 50, 62, 74, 79, geese, 119, 187, Canada geese, 49–51, 53, 116, 119, tundra swan, 61; finch and grosbeaks—cardinal, 48, 65, indigo bunting, 22, 15, 108, goldfinch, 48, house finch, 217, purple finch, 65, rose-breasted grosbeck; flycatcher family—least flycatcher, 48, kingbird, 87, 147, golden-crowned kinglet, 9; grouse and turkey—ruffed grouse, 17, 55–57, 108, wild turkey, 61, 67, 108, 128–31, 147; gulls, 3–4; hawks and eagles—87–89, 111, bald eagle, 61; hummingbird, 8, 80, 81–83, 87; loon, 125–27; moorhen (gallinule), 62, 78; neo-tropical songbirds, 121; nuthatches, 144; owls—great-horned owl, 154, 158, spotted owl, 184; sparrows—133, 145, chipping sparrow, 8, junco, 145, song sparrow, 65, swamp sparrow, 48; scarlet tanager, 100, 108; tern, 62–63; thrasher, 22, 47, 48; thrush family—112, 138, bluebirds, 3, 22, 44, 64, 67, 108, 110, robins, 93, 64–65, 108, 111, 116, 172, 187, veery, 20, 100, wood thrush, 19, 20, 100; vireos—134, red-eyed vireo, 19, 100, warbling vireo, 93; warblers—22–23, 115, 173, 182, Blackburnian warbler, 23, chestnut-sided warbler, 134, redstart, 134, yellowthroat, 134; woodcock, 9, 20; woodpecker family—62, downy woodpecker, 22, flicker, 22, 93, 110, pileated woodpecker, 18, 101, 139, red-bellied woodpecker, 144; wrens, 22, 187
birding, 173
blizzard of 1966, 138
books and periodicals: *National Geographic Magazine,* 124; *NYS Conservationist Magazine,* 124; *Bird Guide* of Chester Reed, 125
Boston, Mass., 33
Boy Scouts of America: and Dan Beard, 10; Green-Bar Bill Hilcourt, 8; Eric Sloan, 10
Brazil, 84
Burgess, Thornton, 150
Burroughs, John, 19, 22

Calaway Gardens, 90
calendar (Gregorian), 15
calico fields, 70–72
camping, 20
carbon dioxide, 168, 175–76
Carson, Rachel, 33
Caumsett Park, Long Island, 150
Central America, 121
Central New York, 67–68, 85
Chase, Marge (newspaper editor), xxi
cheese factory (Rogers Center), 23
chemistry, organic, 165–67
Chenango River, 141–42
chicken, 174
clouds: formation, 10–12; cirrus (wisps), 14, 101; stratus, 37, 64, 101
coal, 187
color in nature: sunrise, 49–50; autumn, 25, 116–18

Columbus, Christopher, 13–14, 33
community, natural, 187
condensation, nuclei of, 11
conservation agencies, 130–31, 178, 184
corn, 188
courtship, 55, 129
Cox, Donald D., 152
crops, 4
cycles in nature, 167

David (king of Israel), 45
death and mortality, 165–67
decomposition, 168
Department of Environmental Conservation, 130–31
depression, national, xvii
deserts, expanding, 177
dewpoint, 11
drainage, 4–5

Earth orbit, 176
ecosystem, 179
Ede, Basil, 111
education, 123
eggs, 47, 61–63; catbird, 48; veery, 100; turkey, 130
Egyptians, ancient, 155
Emerson, Ralph Waldo, 19
emigrants, European, 88
energy: in nature of, 46–48, 159, 165; budgets, 176; change in, 57, 164; distribution of, 176
environmental citizenship, 164; commandments of, 179–80; sanity in, 176–77
equinox, 154–56
excretion, 170

farm habitats, 7–9
feeders, 143–46
Fields, Marshall (estate of), 150
fireplace, 137
Fischer, Richard B., 114
fish: pickerel, 79
fishing, hunting, trapping, 31, 57, 139
Flintham, Stuart, 6, 19
flooding, periodic, 4, 45
flowers, wild. *See* plants
flyways, migration, 119
fog, 50
forest: floor, 120; hardwoods, 128; rainforest, 183
forestry, 184
Franklin, Benjamin, 147
Fuertes, Louis Agassiz, 10

gardening, 77
Gillespie, Ga., xxii
glaciers, 175
goblins, 187
grandchildren, 181
grasses: lawn, 58–60, 132; prairie, 84
greenhouse effect, 175
Groundhog Day, 160–62
growing season, 117

habitat, underwater, 176
Hart's Woods, 19–21
hayfields, 84
hearthside, 139
heat traps, 175
heavens, 37
hedgerow, 13
hormones, 157–59
Hudson's Bay Company, 137
humidity, 11

hunters (deer), 37–40
Hurlbutt, John, xxi

Ice Age, 175–78
immigrants (European), 33, 88, 128
insects: ants, 114; aphid lion (larva of ladybird beetle), 114; aphis, 114; honey bees, 71, 79, 115; beetles, 28, 114; butterflies, 90–92, 115, 122–24; moths, 47
invertebrates: protozoa, 167; balloon spider, 25–28; crab spider, 114; funnel web spider, 25; wasps, 115
Iroquois National Wildlife Refuge, 22

January, 157–59
jobs, 184

Kelly, Jane, xxi
kingbird, 87

Lakes: Adirondack, 126; Central New York, 126; Lake Ontario, 13
land fill, 174
land use change, 3–6
Leopold, Aldo, 45, 49, 174
lifestyle: revolution in, xvii; changes, 174
logging, 184–86

mammals (alien species): fallow deer, 29; red deer, 29; sika deer, 29
mammals (native species): bear family, 34, 141; bison family, 33–36, 84; cat family—lynx, 137, puma, 140; deer family—white-tailed deer, 29, 32, 54, 67, 101, 172–73; dog family—coyotes, 87, foxes, 87–89, 154, 168, wolves, 33–35; rabbits—110, 137, cottontail, 17, 43–44, 48, 87, 116, 172; rodents—meadow vole, 87–89, 116, 142, 159, white-footed mouse, 116, 142, chipmunk, 110, woodchuck, 160–62, shrews, 142; weasel family—87–89, badger, 141, ferrets (pole cats), 141, fisher, 167, marten, 141, mink, 141, otter, 141, short-tailed weasel, 141–42, wolverine, 141
Marcellus and Otisco Railroad, 97
marsh, 77
meadow: sedge, 78; hayfield, 84

Nassau County, 151
naturalists, 19, 165
natural resources, 195
nectar, 115
neo-tropical songbirds, 121
nesting. *See* birds
New England hill farmers, 33
New York City, 33
New York State, 33; Central N.Y., 127; Dept. of Environmental Conservation, 130–31; game farms, 24, 130
nitrates, 168
North America, 121
Nova Scotia, 82
November, 132–43

Oak Orchard Wildlife Management Area, 3
Oak Orchard Creek, 3

oceans: expanding, 177; and underwater habitats, 175
oil, 187
omens, 187
On Golden Pond (film), 125
Onondaga County, 67–69
orchards, 3, 41
Orleans County, 3, 19
oxygen, 176

pastures, tropical, 182
phosphates, 168
photography, 141
photosynthesis, 46–48
pituitary, 157
plains (Lake Ontario), 13
plants (non-flowering), 46–48
plants (flowering herbaceous): alfalfa, 161; amaranth, 133; arrow arum, 113; arrowhead, 78; aster, 74; baneberry, 99; bachelor button, 99; bellflower, 90; black-eyed Susan, 99; bloodroot, 43, 99; buttercup, 71; campion, 70; cardinal flower, 114; cat-tail, 79; chickweed, 72; chicory, 72; clover, 58, 184; cohosh, 9, 70; coltsfoot, 9; coneflower, 99; corn, 60, 113; daisy, 71; dame's rocket, 71; dandelion, 58, 70, 172; day lily, 71; gill-over-the-ground, 71; goldenrod, 74, 114; hawksbeard, 90; hawkweed, 59, 71; orange hawkweed, 58–59; hepatica, 9, 99; joe-pye weed, 77–78; knapweed, 99; lamb's quarters, 79; leek, 9, 99; lizard's tail, 79; lobelia, 99; purple loosestrife, 71; mallow, 71, 104; maple, 14; burr marigold, 112; swamp milkweed, 77; mints, 59, 71; mullein, 90; mustard, 70; oats, 142; pickerelweed, 79; common plantain, 58; pond-weed, 79; Queen-Anne's-lace, 59, 71; common ragweed, 133; giant ragweed, 46; sedges, 78; water smartweed, 79; false Solomon's seal, 99; spring beauty, 9, 43; sunflower, 99; timothy, 142, bird's foot trefoil, 113; trillium, 99; tulip, 172; veronica, 58–60, 71, 172; violet, 58, 70; water lily, 78; wheat, 113, 142; yarrow, 59
plants (trees and shrubs): apples—8, 22–24, 172; thornapple, 134; aspen, 19, 25; beech, 134, 182; blackberry, 134; cherries—110, 172, chokecherry, 8; chestnut, 128; cornels and dogwoods, 70; silky cornel, 70, 172, 113; hawthorns, 133; honey suckle, 111, 113; hop-hornbeam, 20; maples—red maple, 19, 25; sugar maple, 93–95, 96–98, 182; mountainash, 133; red oak, 134; reforestation, 186; shadbush, 172; walnut, 182; black willow, 80
plant succession, 3–6
pollen, 78
prairie grasses, 84
precipitation. *See* rainfall; snow
precocial young, 61
predation, 87–89, 143
productivity, 41–42

rabbits, 110, 137
radiation (heat loss), 175
radio (NPR), 175
railroad, 97
rainfall and leaf fall, 135

rainforest, 183, 185, 192
ranchers, 149
range, breeding, 55
reduction, 176
regeneration, 167
reproduction: of forests, 176; of food supply, 158
reptile, 188
resources, natural, 178, 187–89
respiration, 176
rights, constitutional, 187
roadside nature watching, 18, 67–69
rocks, 187–89
Rogers Environmental Education Center, 131
Roosevelt, Franklin D., 38
runoff, 4

sailboats, toy, 5
sand, 187
scavenging, 149
Sherburne, N.Y., 131
shrubs. *See* plants (trees and shrubs)
skiing, 16–18, 139
Smith, Greg, 107–9
Smith, Janet J., xxii
snow, 16–18
snowshoeing, 139
soil, earth, 195, 187–88
solar year, 154
solstice, 156
South America, 121
spirits, 187
spring, 41–42, 43–45, 46–48, 157–59, 187
starvation, 47–48
summer, 74–75
sun, 154; at sunrise, 13–15, 49; at sunset, 43–44

survival, 47–48
synthesis, 167

teacher workshops, 114
teaching, 137
television, 173
temperature, 175; cooling, 137–39, 175; heating, 175
territory and migration, 55
Thoreau, Henry David, xvii, 19
thunderstorms, 11
tracks, tracking: fox, 15; skunk, 15; cottontail, 15, 17; pheasant, 17
trees: diameter, 96; wind resistance, 97; energy flow, 98. *See also* plants (trees and shrubs)

Uncle Remus, 150
Urquhart, Fred A. and Norah, 122
United States Forest Service, 178, 184; Dept. of Interior, 178; Dept. of Agriculture, 178
Utica College, 184

walking, hiking: on the home farm, 7–9; at the Rogers Center, 136–38
Washington, D.C., 33
water, 95
weather fronts, 11
weeds, 69–71
Weeks family: Brenda (daughter), xxii; Dorothy (sister), xxii; Edwin J. (father), xvii, 181; Edwin T. (brother), xix, 19–21; Eleanore Wilder (sister), xvii; Esther (Bulmore) Weeks (wife), xxii, 94; John A. (author), 131; Joni Weeks

Dyer (daughter), xxii, 1, 41, 103, 135, 163; Mary Eugenia (Jean) Stetson (sister), xvii; Sarah A. (mother), xvii, 44, 116–17; Wilfred (brother), xvii
wildlife: farm, 4; forest, 128
winter, 135, 137–39, 157–59
woodlots, 13
WRVO staff, xxi

xanthophyll, 133

Youth Conservation Corps, 19–21

zealots, 185